High-Speed Empire
Chinese Expansion and the Future of Southeast Asia

COLUMBIA GLOBAL REPORTS
NEW YORK

High-Speed Empire

Chinese Expansion
and the Future
of Southeast Asia

Will Doig

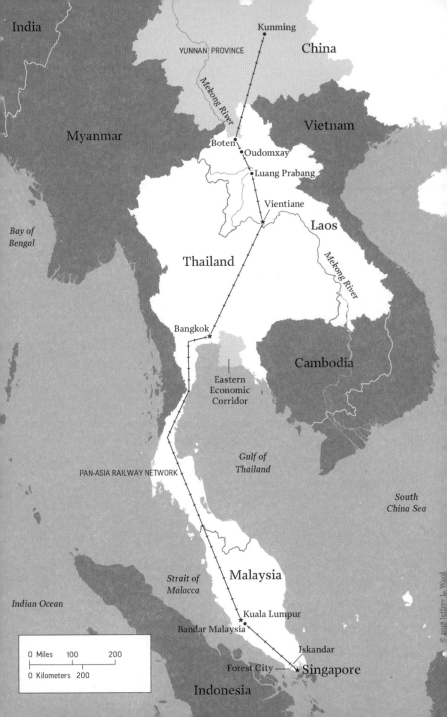

High-Speed Empire
Chinese Expansion and the Future of Southeast Asia

Published by Columbia Global Reports
91 Claremont Avenue, Suite 515
New York, NY 10027
globalreports.columbia.edu
facebook.com/columbiaglobalreports
@columbiaGR

Library of Congress Control Number: 2018935104
ISBN: 978-0997722987

Book design by Strick&Williams
Map design by Jeffrey L. Ward
Author photograph by Adam Arjuna

Printed in the United States of America

For Jim Doig

CONTENTS

Introduction

In 1991, when Shanghai decided to build a subway, the World Bank scolded it for "opting for such an expensive system as metro without studying all possible alternatives." This was, after all, a city of 6.5 million bicycles and less than 200,000 motor vehicles, most of which were commercial trucks and buses. Might the city be better off improving its bike infrastructure instead? "It is doubtful that such an expensive mode can be the core to the urban transport system for passengers," the bank concluded.

Shanghai decided to build a subway anyway. In fact, the city had already broken ground on a system a quarter-century earlier when, in 1964, its Tunnel Engineering Bureau dug a prototype 2,100-foot tunnel and metro station deep below Hengshan Park in the French Concession. The project was shelved a few years later amid the mayhem of the Cultural Revolution, but in January 1990 the State Council greenlit a fresh plan, and work began anew.

The Shanghai subway project represented a major public
works contract, and firms from a dozen countries bid to have
a hand in building it. For the next five years, 10,000 workers
bored through Shanghai's claylike soil. "Shanghai, it seems, is
eager to play catch-up with the rest of the world," wrote the *New
York Times*.

That it was. On April 10, 1995, Shanghai inaugurated its first
full metro line, a state-of-the-art ten miles of tunnel and thir-
teen stations. At the People's Square stop, officials unfurled a
red carpet. One Hong Kong developer marveled that the nimble
process was "actually less bureaucratic" than in the United
States. Agog at its own strength, Shanghai set the ambitious
goal of expanding the system to two hundred miles of track by
2045, a full fifty years in the future.

It beat its own deadline by decades. Today, over 400 miles
in length, the Shanghai Metro is the world's longest subway
system, carrying more than three billion passengers each year.

These kinds of colossal infrastructure projects have become
marketing devices for China's unstoppability. Forty years ago,
the country's transportation infrastructure coverage was among
the sparsest in the world. Today, nearly 2.5 million miles of
roads branch out across its provinces. In 2011, the length of
China's expressways surpassed the U.S. Interstate Highway
System's. Ten of the world's top twenty container ports are in
China, including the biggest, in Shanghai. In 2015, the government announced its intention to build forty new airports in the
next five years. This breakneck mentality propels the private
sector as well. Last year, a Changsha-based real estate developer

14   built a fifty-seven-story skyscraper in nineteen days, simply because he could.

The crown jewel of these ventures is China's high-speed rail system, constructed in the space of about a decade, and bigger than any other high-speed system in the world. The network's first train rolled from Beijing to Tianjin on August 1, 2008, days before the opening ceremonies of the Summer Games in Beijing. Eight years later, China Railway announced its high-speed network had surpassed the 20,000 kilometer mark, then projected it to extend beyond 45,000 kilometers by 2030.

Since then, China's most visible railway endeavors haven't even been in China itself. A major thrust of the country's economic strategy involves building infrastructure beyond its own borders. Many of these efforts fall under its One Belt One Road initiative, China's plan to pull half the globe into its orbit with an interconnected network of roads, rail, airports, and seaports. The plan has become its own brand—on my Cathay Pacific flight to Hong Kong, the seatback TV played Bank of China ads offering to connect me to "One Belt One Road opportunities." It's on freeway billboards in Bangkok and front-page news in Vientiane. Maps of the initiative show arrows criss-crossing the earth, from Asia to Africa to Europe. Many of the countries in the path of these routes can't build such infrastructure themselves, and see China's offers to build it for them as a chance to leapfrog up the development chain.

The "Belt" refers to the Silk Road Economic Belt, an overland network of infrastructure, supply chains, and trading routes stretching from China to Western Europe. The "Road" is the

Twenty-first Century Maritime Silk Road, a web of shipping lanes traversing the Indian Ocean, Persian Gulf, and Mediterranean Sea. Taken together, it's a scheme of surreal scope, even for China. Yet it's not a cohesive plan so much as a well-funded idea that could manifest in various ways. It includes pools of financial backing for transport, energy, and urbanization projects, and a mandate to form economic partnerships and liberalize cross-border trade. It's also evolved as a bid to counterbalance American influence in the region, and a marketing slogan to brand China as the world's premiere global developer.

Though only officially launched by Chinese President Xi Jinping in 2013, the effort has quickly become the country's marquee initiative. In February 2016, a freight train rolled from China to Iran for the first time, a 6,462-mile journey through oil- and gas-rich Central Asia. On the Indian Subcontinent, China is developing a corridor of roads, rail, and energy infrastructure linking Pakistan's coast to the western Chinese territory of Xinjiang. One Belt One Road now includes a Turkish seaport bought by Chinese state-owned companies, an industrial park in Belarus, and a railway from Nairobi to the Kenyan coast. Encompassing more than sixty countries and over a trillion dollars in spending, the Belt and Road Initiative is an endeavor to make China an epicenter of global commercial activity.

As far as China is concerned, this is simply a return to the natural order, the end of a long and embarrassing losing streak that shouldn't have occurred in the first place. This is what Xi means when he talks about the "Chinese Dream"—not Herbert

16 Hoover's "a chicken in every pot and a car in every garage," but the return of a Middle Kingdom to be reckoned with. Just as China sits at the center of the world map that hangs in Beijing's Foreign Ministry, One Belt One Road is a plan to reclaim the country's global centrality, with the hardware of its worldwide trade stretching across Asia, Africa, and Europe, all of it ultimately flowing back to the People's Republic.

One of the initiative's many tentacles looks tantalizingly within reach.

The Pan-Asia Railway was first proposed at the 1995 ASEAN Summit as a regionwide network of rail connections running from China to Singapore. Political disagreements and a lack of funds stalled the project until the early 2000s when China, by then a leader in global development, began making efforts to jump-start it. Like One Belt One Road itself, the Pan-Asia Railway is more an idea than a cohesive plan, with proposed links serving different purposes depending on the country they run through. It's a piecemeal process slowly unfolding through bilateral agreements hammered out case by case, making its diplomatic hurdles at least as daunting as its actual construction.

The railway would begin in Kunming, capital of Yunnan, the far southwestern province that forms China's border with Southeast Asia. From there, China envisions the tracks diving southward, crossing into Laos at the abandoned city of Boten, and working its way down the peninsula through Laos, Thailand, and Malaysia, before terminating on the island of Singapore.

The notion of a train from China to Singapore has been on
the drawing board for over a century. In 1904, the Trans-Siberian
Railway connected Moscow to the Pacific, and soon afterward,
British and French colonists began pondering their own grand
railroad that would weave together their tropical trophies on the
Indochina peninsula. They came close to realizing the dream
with a meter-gauge track that would have run all the way from
Kunming to Singapore if not for a missing link between Saigon
and Phnom Penh. But when the colonial powers departed, the
will to unify the region left with them, proving the railway
dream was always as much about fortifying an empire as providing transportation.

Throughout the twentieth century, the colonial railways of
Southeast Asia heroically trundled along, gradually falling apart
and occasionally bombed to bits. Meanwhile, China knitted
together its own far-flung provinces with a massive network of
tracks Paul Theroux dubbed the Iron Rooster. It was a dreary
time for the Middle Kingdom. Its losses in the Opium Wars had
plunged it into a prolonged foul mood that China itself called
its "Century of Humiliation," a period during which dominant
foreign powers demanded concessions that essentially transferred elements of Chinese national sovereignty to its Western
adversaries. Shanghai, Guangzhou, and other Chinese ports
were forced to open to foreign trade, and British subjects were
granted extraterritoriality privileges while staying in China. In
major Chinese cities, Western and Japanese powers established
insular settlements, isolating themselves from Chinese society
in Epcot-style replicas of home.

18   The Century of Humiliation became a motivating propellant, eventually used by the Communist Party to whip up a nationalistic commitment to strengthening and growth. One Belt One Road is this commitment made manifest, as is the Pan-Asia Railway, which would fuse China with the Southeast Asian up-and-comers it has far surpassed in power. Some of these countries, like Thailand and Malaysia, have growing consumer classes hungry for Chinese exports. Others, like Myanmar, funnel resources like jade and natural gas to China. Many of them have strategically located seaports. Others have potential as real estate frontiers where Chinese developers can build cities to which Chinese expats can flock. In return for the access, China is offering what amounts to a once-in-a-lifetime deal: a significant chunk of the annual $1.7 trillion in infrastructure developing Asia needs to build between now and 2030.

No country has less of this infrastructure than Laos. By fate of geography, the tiny communist state finds itself at the center of the drama, with the giant on its northern border requesting permission to barrel through. Laos is awash in natural resources like timber and minerals—resources a railway could haul back to China by the trainload. It also has an abundance of water. The Mekong River and its tributaries nurture Laos's farms and hydropower plants with more water resources per capita than any other country in Asia.

So rarely regarded is Laos that when President Obama visited in 2016 the U.S. Embassy in Vientiane spent a year meticulously preparing for his drop in. Laos's most valuable contribution to the Pan-Asia Railway might simply be a path southward. "The quality that has long defined Laos is how its location has always made it susceptible to outside influences," says Frank Albert, a former U.S. State Department official who worked in Laos in the 1960s and maintains personal ties to the country. French colonialists saw Laos as a buffer to hold back the British. The Vietnamese used it as a bulwark against the Chinese. The U.S. saw it as a firewall to keep communism from spilling into Thailand, and the Viet Cong used Laos as a pass-through to shuttle supplies to its troops in South Vietnam. In his book *A Great Place to Have a War*, Joshua Kurlantzick, a senior fellow at the Council on Foreign Relations and a leading authority on the region, writes that Dwight D. Eisenhower was so obsessed with Laos as a barrier to communism's spread that he warned John F. Kennedy that its security was the most pressing foreign policy issue in the world.

Now Laos's location has once again made it a place worth engaging, a place to which China has routinely dispatched delegates bearing enticing promises and subtle threats. "It's almost a call-and-response thing," says Brian Eyler, who spent fifteen years working in China and is now director of the Southeast Asia program at the Stimson Center, a Washington think tank. "We're not really sure what the outcome will be. What we're sure of is that China is not going away."

Welcome to Laos Vegas

The Royal Jingland Hotel, boomerang-shaped and painted gold, presided over the tiny city of Boten like a pair of arms spread wide. Years ago, arriving guests, mostly Chinese, followed a red carpet into its smoky lobby and queued up at a reception desk to the left. After checking in, many quickly made their way to the baccarat tables in the casino. Others were intercepted by the prostitutes who went room to room pitching their services. Out front, electric trams idled near the fountain, waiting to shuttle guests to the city's throbbing dive bars, velvet-rope nightclubs, and street vendors selling Chinese aphrodisiacs and pirated DVDs.

The 270-room hotel was well known in Boten's gaudy little kingdom of clubs, drugs, casinos, hookers, and crime both petty and organized. Gambling is illegal in China, a nuisance that Boten beat on a technicality by existing just over the border in Laos. But though it was in Laos, Boten was essentially a Chinese city. Chinese nationals enjoyed relaxed visa requirements, and constituted virtually the entire labor force. In front of Boten's shops, barking vendors with Yunnanese accents hawked replica Jimmy Choo pumps. The streets were patrolled not by Laotian police but by security forces on China's payroll. Even the clocks were set to Beijing time, an hour ahead of Vientiane. (The lady-boys, bused in from Thailand, provided the only heterogeneity.)

A mere six square miles, or a bit smaller than New York's John F. Kennedy Airport, Boten itself was a Chinese import, made possible under the auspices of the Boten Special Economic Zone. The SEZ, established jointly in 2003 between the Chinese government and the Laos Ministry of Planning and Investment, effectively handed Boten to China in its entirety. The Lao villagers who originally lived there were quickly relocated several miles down the road, and a development entity called the Fok Hing Company from Hong Kong acquired a thirty-year lease to develop the city. A diplomatic cable from the time indicates that the U.S. State Department suspected this company might be "a front organization" for Boten's principal investor, a Mr. Huang Ming Xian. A Fujianese businessman with reported links to a similar casino enterprise in Myanmar, Huang spent tens of millions of dollars building the sleazy gambling outpost in the Lao wilderness. One brochure described Boten as "a golden place hiding in the luxuriant jungles, just like Peter Pan's city of never falling down, just like mysterious treasure island." An ad in a tourism magazine called it the "most internationally modernized city in Laos," which wasn't far from the truth, though it was modernized by another country entirely.

22   For several years, Boten's garish amusements attracted thousands of Chinese tourists. But as the decade wore on, the city's patina began to show. Overwhelmed Lao immigration officials started losing their grip on the border as unruly visitors, rightly thinking of Boten as China's personal property, would blow through the checkpoint from Yunnan province with impunity, their SUVs kicking up dust as they sped into Laos uninspected. Gamblers who couldn't make good on their losses began vanishing, and in 2009, officials from China's Hubei province rushed to the border to negotiate the release of a group of Chinese tourists held hostage in the back of one of the casinos. Corpses with gunshot wounds began turning up in alleys, and rumors spread that the hills around Boten were filled with shallow graves.

Finally, in 2010, the Chinese foreign ministry had to warn tourists to avoid Boten's unsavory venues, terminating the town's only reason for existing. In March the next year, Beijing decided the fun was over and ended the visa exemption for Chinese citizens. It even cut the city's power and cell phone signal. One month later, the Royal Jingland Hotel rolled up its red carpet, parked the trams in the weeds behind the building, and slapped a bike lock on its doors.

The city's ridiculous rise and collapse became another curious byproduct of China's hyperactive growth. But Boten was not originally meant to be just a gambling town. Boten Golden City was supposed to be exactly what its official designation suggested: a special economic zone that could function as China's gateway into Southeast Asia. The original

plans included a trading center, a manufacturing complex, and   23
storage facilities—the infrastructural support for a waystation
linking neighboring regional economies. Boten collapsed before
it could fully cash in on the one thing it had going for it—its
border crossing, connecting one of the world's most powerful
nations to one of the least.

Just beyond the Boten border crossing is the beginning of Route
3 in Laos. For decades, Route 3 was a crumbling blacktop, and
before that, an opium smuggling trail. With fortitude, time, and
four-wheel drive, you could follow this road straight through
Laos's mountains to the Thai border. If you wanted, you could
continue to Bangkok, keep driving down the turquoise coast
into Malaysia and right through Kuala Lumpur, and end up in
downtown Singapore.

In the early 2000s, the network of roads to which Route 3
belongs were rebuilt, resurfaced, and modernized. The Asian
Development Bank managed the project and provided the loans,
but China, which stood to benefit from the improved access,
directly financed chunks of it. "China to Build Highway to Link
China and Thailand," reported the *People's Daily* in 2002, the
headline failing to even mention little Laos, the country the
road would actually run through.

To connect its own cities to this network, China also spent
$4 billion improving the road from Kunming to Boten, which
was in nearly as poor condition as Route 3 itself. "Half the people
were throwing up" by the time they arrived at the Laos border,
joked one Yunnan official. Workers blasted the road through

24 the Himalayan foothills. One treacherous stretch required 430 bridges. When all was said and done, the 1,150-mile river of asphalt flowed all the way to Bangkok.

It was one of China's earlier feats of strength, announcing the country's arrival in Southeast Asia, a region in which its presence would grow increasingly visible in the years that followed. In 1992, trade between Cambodia, Laos, Thailand, Myanmar, Vietnam, and the Chinese regions of Yunnan and Guangxi amounted to $37 billion annually. By 2005, it had exploded to $154 billion.

As for little Boten, its brush with fame as a swinging party town had occurred purely by luck of location as the first Southeast Asian village on the Kunming-Bangkok Expressway. When China walked away from the city in 2011, Boten became a place without a purpose. Its few remaining residents buzzed through the empty streets on sputtering motorbikes. Some ran tin-box shops built into the sides of the former tourist traps, their Mandarin signage betraying the identities of Boten's original pioneers. In the afternoon sun, they would dry maize on the concrete pavilion of an abandoned nightclub called Super Star. The club itself was corn yellow, and fronted with smoked-glass windows, Corinthian columns, and sun-bleached posters showing attractive young Chinese revelers drinking expensive-looking cocktails and having the time of their lives.

Its pastel buildings peeling and cracking in Laos's subtropical heat, for five years Boten sat silently in the jungle, waiting for a new band of settlers to return with the next big idea.

*

In a brand new stadium in the Laotian capital of Vientiane on December 12, 2009, Phouthavong Outhasak knelt before his coach, gently bowed, and touched his forehead to the ground. It was day four of the twenty-fifth annual Southeast Asian Games, and the local martial arts fighter had just bested his Cambodian opponent in the taekwondo finals. In the stands, the local crowd was uproarious, chanting, "Lao, su, su!" ("Laos, fight, fight!") in a display of unchecked exuberance rarely seen in this soft-spoken country. But tonight was different. Hosting the games for the first time, Team Laos was on track to win thirty-three gold medals, crushing its previous record of five in 2007. After bowing to his coach, Phouthavong rose with tears in his eyes and tied the Lao flag around his neck, then screamed in triumph at the crowd, which responded with a roar that shook the stands. He then scaled the grandstand and approached not his father, nor his mother, but Laos's deputy prime minister, Somsavat Lengsavad.

It was a moment of glory for Somsavat, too. The Southeast Asian Games were a big deal for Laos, probably the most elaborate state event the country had ever held. Somsavat had led the organizing committee, and now his efforts were paying off spectacularly. Every time the announcers mentioned his name, the crowd of spectators cheered with approval. Draped in a shimmering white jacket, the dapper statesman beamed from the stands, presiding over what was turning out to be quite a triumph for a country not accustomed to winning much of anything.

The Games were Laos's debut on the regional stage, and they were also Somsavat's. He was developing an enviable reputation

26 in the Politburo of the People's Revolutionary Party as a man who could get things built. The stadium for the Games was constructed by a consortium of Chinese companies through a backroom agreement devised over two years earlier by Somsavat. At the meeting, the leader of the China Development Bank offered to build the $100 million facility on one condition: In return, Laos would have to give China a separate plot of land nearby to develop. The two men agreed on a muddy 4,000-acre patch in northeast Vientiane called the That Luang marsh.

The That Luang marsh provided sustenance for seventeen Lao villages, whose residents harvested snails from its brackish waters and rice from its swampy soil. After the stadium deal, the government rebranded That Luang the "New City Development Project," but everyone knew what it really was: a Chinatown shoehorned into the nation's capital. Rumors swirled that soon, something would rise there, something Chinese—perhaps it would be monolithic condo towers, chintzy malls, or a hulking, insular city—and that Somsavat's deal included a concession to allow 50,000 Chinese citizens to move into the development, which provoked a rare outcry from the Lao public. Equally rare was Somsavat's impulse to explain himself. At a press conference in February 2008, he insisted there would be "no discrimination among buyers and no special concessions for Chinese citizens." It did not help that Somsavat is ethnically Chinese and was educated in a Chinese primary school. He downplays his Mandarin fluency, but it's serviceable enough that he can use it to cut deals with Beijing officials.

Somsavat held a second press conference in March to con-
tain the That Luang fallout, but the protests continued, per-
mitted, perhaps, because sections of the marsh were owned
by Party members themselves. The That Luang complex was
downsized in 2010, and today, a string of nineteen-story-tall
flamingo-pink condominiums, built by the Shanghai Wan Feng
Real Estate Company, are rising on the 900-acre site. The struc-
tures, encircling a manmade lake, shimmer in the humid air like
sentinels watching over the villagers who tend to the marsh's
remaining rice paddies. The complex is an anomaly in low-rise
Vientiane, cut off from the city by all but a few access roads.
Upscale retail shops, an entertainment complex, and a theme
park are said to be planned for the future.

The stadium deal, from beginning to end, was straight out
of the Laos development playbook, in which officials bargain
away bits of the country in exchange for foreign-built projects.
Somsavat was the Politburo's savviest player of this game; it's
safe to say that no other Lao politician has brought more foreign development to Laos in such a short time. In this respect,
he personifies what many in Southeast Asia today both yearn
for and fear: the heavy hand of China reaching deep into their
countries, bearing expensive gifts and offers one can't refuse,
but also a rising level of Chinese visibility that stirs up concerns about sovereignty and identity. "China has significant
influence because of the investments they've made, but it's still
a love-hate relationship," says Ian Baird, a leading Laos expert
at the University of Wisconsin-Madison. For poorer Southeast

28 Asian countries looking for large-scale infrastructure, China is often the best option. "If you wait for other people to come in and build this stuff, it will never happen," says the Asia Institute Tasmania's James Chin. "Only the Chinese can do it quickly."

No one subscribed to this theory more fervently than Somsavat Lengsavad. A self-fashioned Lao Robert Moses with dreams bigger than his cash-strapped nation could afford, he saw China as the quickest path to building the highways, railways, and hydroelectric dams he believed could finally tether Laos's fortunes to the Southeast Asian economic miracle. "Laos has always been a zone of contention," says the Stimson Center's Brian Eyler. "There are leaders that are closer to Vietnam, to Thailand, to China. But of those that are close to China, Somsavat has always been the closest of them all."

Born and raised in the former Lao capital of Luang Prabang, Somsavat came of age in the 1950s during Laos's postcolonial transition. The French hadn't left much behind. When the Royal Lao Government took power in 1953, Laos had barely a hundred registered vehicles and the Mekong River was still its main transit artery. Another decade would pass before phone service would connect the provincial centers. For many Lao, life continued as it had for centuries, supplemented by airlifted sacks of bulgur from the United States.

The new government relied heavily on American aid, and many Lao feared and resented the visible presence of a new Western power just as the old one was departing. Vietnamese communists exploited this skepticism and began spreading

their political ideology across the border. By 1955, Laos had its　29
own communist party. In the years that followed, communist
Lao guerrillas, backed by the Viet Minh, fought skirmishes with
the American-supported Royal Lao Army in the country's north
and east. As Laos was pulled into the Vietnam War, these guer-
rilla fighters grew into an organized force, a communist insurgency known as the Pathet Lao that was effectively commanded
by the North Vietnamese.

By the mid 1960s the Pathet Lao controlled access to half the
country, and within this territory, it educated Lao youth on the
dangers of foreign influence and liberal democracy. Somsavat
was one of these youths. The revolutionary talk appealed to
his rebellious teenage spirit, and with a group of his classmates
he dropped out of school to fight for Laos's "independence." By
his mid-teens he had become an enthusiastic revolutionary,
trading fire with government forces in the caves of the country's
communist-controlled north. He was also an instinctual leader,
organizing village- and district-level militias, and regaling the
peasantry with nationalistic tales of the injustices that foreigners had perpetrated upon the Lao people. At nineteen, he
was appointed secretary to Kaysone Phomvihane, the revolutionary movement's commander. When Kaysone seized power
in 1975, Somsavat found himself working for the new prime
minister of Laos.

Once in office, the fledgling communist regime set about
slicing the country into agricultural collectives, which it
believed would be more productive and more susceptible to cen-
tralized control. From the start, however, the collectives were a

30   failure, and by 1979 the government was already permitting certain forms of capitalistic enterprise to stabilize the economy. These reforms occurred just as Deng Xiaoping was liberalizing China's economy as well, and though Sino-Vietnamese tensions prevented Laos from enjoying intimate ties with China, Deng's reforms surely influenced Laos's. In 1989, Kaysone visited Beijing—the first head of state to do so after the Tienanmen Square massacre. The visit seemed to signal Laos's desire to shore up ties to its communist neighbors as the Soviet Union teetered.

Meanwhile, Somsavat began his ascent, becoming deputy prime minister in 1998. His name soon became synonymous with Laos's proliferating foreign-built infrastructure. He negotiated deals to put hydropower dams on the Mekong, advancing Laos's long-term goal of becoming the "battery of Southeast Asia," an economic strategy befitting a landlocked country bisected by a powerful river. Laos's goal was to get its hydropower generation capacity up to 12,000 megawatts by 2020, then double that by 2030, and export 80 percent of the energy.

Somsavat was also the closest thing the grim-faced Politburo had to a humanizing emissary, and was often dispatched to grin at public events and jabber at the state-controlled press corps. But the genial front he presented to the public masked a belligerent, battle-hardened brawler. He once upbraided his interpreter in front of fifty people for daring to sit while he was standing. Journalists who deigned to ask questions that strayed from the slow-pitch formula faced his wrath; he once wrapped up a press conference by shouting at the media, "If I wasn't the best, I would not be the boss!" In 2009, at an organizing meeting

for the Southeast Asian Games, he lashed out at the head of
the National Sports Committee, asking, "Has the committee
brought a punching bag for the boxers? If not, they can use the
chairman instead."

In a society where causing others to lose face is a paramount sin, Somsavat's aggressive nature was jarring. It was
also remarkably effective at producing results. In clearing the
way for development, he was pushing against the headwinds
of history, which for centuries have largely held Laos at arm's
length from Southeast Asia's economic climb. In the 1300s,
Laos was an insular kingdom known as Lan Xang that failed to
collect the taxes that could have funded public works projects
and city-building initiatives. It missed out on the economic
evolutions brought to its coastal neighbors by seafaring European traders. When the French colonized the country, it left it
neglected, and Laos further stagnated.

Today, Laos's cryptic and paranoid Politburo is the reason
the country has few NGOs, and its English-language news-
paper, *The Vientiane Times*, is a broadsheet of pure propaganda.
Foreign journalists in Laos often enter as tourists and work
under the radar. Public dissent is rare, and those who choose
to speak up risk fearsome retribution. In 2012, the country's
best-known human rights activist, Sombath Somphone, vanished at a police checkpoint. The subtext of his disappearance
was clear: Don't confuse economic openness with the freedom
to speak your mind.

The country's historical inertia has been due, in part, to its
hobbling lack of connective infrastructure. It has no ports and

32   no freeways comparable to other Southeast Asian nations. To
       remedy this, under leaders like Somsavat, Laos has increasingly
       courted the global market and made "development" the defining
       touchstone of the People's Revolutionary Party.

       Laos is a country that, practically speaking, has no railway.
       Its lone train service is a toylike locomotive that plies a two-mile
       track at a distinctly Lao-like pace. It is essentially just a stub, a
       rickety extension of the Thai rail network that, on the Laos side
       of the border, ends abruptly in a dusty field a dozen miles short
       of Vientiane. Even tiny Djibouti, Luxembourg, Fiji, Nauru, and
       St. Kitts and Nevis have more railways.

       It's been nearly a century since anyone attempted to build
       a proper railway in Laos. In the 1920s, France began planning
       one that would have connected the country to Vietnam's Quang
       Binh province. The goal was to encourage Vietnamese migration
       into its sparsely populated colony to the west. But the Great
       Depression forced France to cancel the project, and it was never
       revived.

       In the early 2000s, when China began plotting its own Lao
       railway, this time linking Kunming with Vientiane, the goal was
       to access Laos's natural resources and connect Yunnan Province
       to the Thai border. In 2009, China and Laos agreed to pursue the
       project, and on April 7, 2010, signed a memorandum of under-
       standing setting the Kunming-Vientiane Railway in motion.

       The project suffered setbacks from the get-go. Less than a
       year after the signing, Liu Zhijun, the Chinese minister of rail-
       ways who had executed the MoU on behalf of Beijing, was fired
       for corruption. "Frankly speaking, the ministerial reshuffle has

slowed down the project," Somsavat said, while also admitting that a series of social and environmental impact studies "didn't meet our expectations." A few months later, a high-speed train collision in the Chinese suburb of Wenzhou killed forty people, raising doubts about the safety of China's railways.

Somsavat was undeterred. Fresh off his successful stadium collaboration with China, he continued to champion the railway, and in 2012 convened a special session of Laos's National Assembly to rubber-stamp the scheme. He even talked up the project with media outlets outside Laos's censorship bubble. "It will boost the Lao economy because many investors are now looking for a production base here," he told Japan's *Nikkei Asian Review*. "They say that if the country had a railway, it would help them reduce their transportation costs. So it would make us more attractive to investors."

Not everyone would benefit, however. The railway would require nearly 10,000 acres of land, displacing over 4,400 Lao families, a Lao official told Radio Free Asia. Laos's deputy minister of public works and transport said the central government was working with provincial task forces to compensate the uprooted residents, but some who had already given up their homes to make way for the project still hadn't been compensated months later, and were skeptical they'd ever be reimbursed for the full value of their properties.

A made-to-order railway would fulfill Laos's dream of going from landlocked to "land-linked," a phrase uttered endlessly by Lao officials promoting the scheme. The deal established a joint

34   venture company to finance the project. China holds 70 percent of this company, and Laos holds the remaining 30 percent. The total budget for the railway is about $6 billion, pared down from an original estimate of $7 billion, a figure analysts had already considered to be extremely optimistic. Of this $6 billion, the initial investment will be just over $2 billion, of which China will contribute about $1.6 billion. Laos will cover the rest.

Laos, however, has nowhere near that kind of cash lying around, so it will borrow most of its share of the cost from China. A website for the Lao-China Railway Company stated in May 2017 that the interest rate for this loan would be 2.3 percent, though people with knowledge of the deal previously pegged it at closer to 3 percent. Even at the 2.3 percent rate, however, the total $6 billion cost of the project would equal nearly half of Laos's entire GDP, and could hobble the country with inescapable debt and complicate access to future financing for more pressing needs.

The debt-heavy railway is oddly out of character, since Laotian bureaucrats run the country with a Depression-era mentality. Laos's fear of debt is understandable. At one point in 2015, the government had less than two months of foreign currency reserves, and has occasionally been unable to pay its civil servants on time. Even banks in Laos are wary of parting with cash. When I tried to withdraw 600 U.S. dollars at the biggest bank in Vientiane, the manager first tried to talk me out of it, then agreed to give me half.

Instead, development in Laos is often done through "build-operate-transfer" arrangements, in which a foreign entity builds infrastructure in Laos, then reaps its profits for a set number of years. After an agreed upon timeframe, the infrastructure is then handed over to the Lao government. Such arrangements have financed the building of multiple dams on the Mekong River and its tributaries.

Laos's willingness to take on such a large amount of debt to build the railway is most plausibly explained by its desperate need for infrastructure, by Somsavat's personal ambition, and by the deals behind the deal—the palm-greased scaffolding that supports many of the major projects of Laos's industrial development complex. "There are leaders in Laos who were put in place and are held there by China's checkbook diplomacy," says one expert on Lao politics. "You have vice ministers in the Lao government for whom China has paid two or three million dollars. China bankrolls their salaries, too. You have that level of involvement, and it feeds and sustains these alliances."

China supplements these kickbacks with regular drop-ins that "don't just flatter Lao officials—concrete things get exchanged between Chinese and Lao delegates at these meetings," according to a foreign diplomat. Laos's mix of political secrecy and liberal economics makes it prone to corruption. In an opaque system controlled by a powerful few, the type of market economy that earns kudos from Western leaders also paves the way for crony capitalism. According to the EU-backed GAN Business Anti-Corruption Portal, over nine million acres of Laotian land have been transferred to private companies since 2000, much of it in deals "made possible by corruption in the land administration and among politicians."

36   The rot runs deep enough that the government's own State Inspection Authority released a report showing corruption had cost Laos $120 million between 2012 and 2014, with millions of it embezzled by ministries and provincial-level offices. In response, the regime embarked on a Beijing-style anti-corruption drive, investigating bureaucrats for graft and publicly auctioning off the Mercedes and BMWs owned by party apparatchiks, who now drive Toyota Camrys instead.

Transparency International rewarded the cleanup campaign in 2016 by ranking Laos the world's fifty-first most corrupt state. (A decade earlier it was in the top 10.) And yet, thanks to a placating growth rate of 7 percent and a ban on free speech, impropriety continues to flourish, and with it, development projects of questionable worth.

"All of us know how corrupt the government is, but we only talk about it in our cars and our flats," a chatty Vientiane taxi driver told me in a rare display of armchair political commentary. "Lao people are like mice who all agree they need to put a bell on the local cat. But for the plan to work, one mouse has to put the bell around the cat's neck, and in Laos, no one will volunteer."

December 2015 marked forty years of one-party rule in the Lao PDR, and to celebrate its streak, the People's Revolutionary Party scheduled three big events. First, it flooded the capital's streets with forty-eight "inspiring parades," during which, as the *Vientiane Times* reported, "all Lao hearts were beating with national pride." Second, it launched Laos's first satellite,

LaoSat-1, a telecommunications orbital designed to improve
connectivity across the country's sparsely populated landscape.

And third, it held a groundbreaking for the railway. Five
years had elapsed since Laos had signed the agreement with
China. When the big day finally arrived, leaders from both countries stood before a row of earth-movers built by LiuGong, the
Chinese heavy-machinery company, and pushed shovels into
ankle-high pyramids of sand. At a canopied booth, delegates
tittered over model trains and glossy renderings.

With these events, the *Vientiane Times* reported, "Laos
trumpeted its success to the world." But the extravaganza
also threw into relief an uncomfortable reality for the ruling
regime. The satellite and the railway were really more China's
achievements than Laos's. China financed and built LaoSat-1
to the tune of $259 million, launched it from Sichuan Prov-
ince, and owns 55 percent of it even as it orbits Earth. As for
the railway, for all the talk of it being a Sino-Lao joint venture, it's always been more geared toward China's needs. For
China, an export-oriented country with a ballooning tourist
class, a railway to ship goods and people southward seems to
make sense. But Laos doesn't export much, and what little it
does mainly comes out of Savannakhet Province, where companies like Toyota and Nikon have manufacturing bases—and
where the railway won't run.

At the time of the fortieth anniversary, members of the
Politburo were asking themselves how much they want China
involved in their matters. Seven weeks after the groundbreaking,
they answered this question at the government's tenth party

38   congress. Staged at the Lao National Convention Center amid flag-festooned parades, 685 delegates representing over 200,000 party members reshuffled the Politburo. When they were finished, the three members representing its most fervently pro-Chinese wing were out: the prime minister, the general secretary, and Somsavat Lengsavad. Elevated to general secretary was a seventy-eight-year-old party stalwart named Bounnhang Vorachit, who was seen as more oriented toward Vietnam, where he received his military training as a youth.

The shakeup's message was clear. China had gotten too close, the party had decided, and China's enablers, Somsavat chief among them, had to go. Despite their proximity and shared communist heritage, China and Laos have a checkered history. In the 1980s, Beijing supported an insurgency in Laos, training combatants in China and sending them back with AK-47s to fight the Lao government. Laos shares far more with Thailand in terms of culture, religion, and language. And historically, its most intimate ally has long been Vietnam, the birthplace of the Pathet Lao. Back in the Kaysone days, Vietnam and Laos were so enmeshed that some Lao leaders identified as both Lao and Vietnamese, toggling between personas to suit the situation at hand.

Laos doesn't make a big decision without first considering how Hanoi might feel about it. Vietnam rivals China as Laos's biggest foreign investor, and it is a fierce China skeptic, as well. A massive railway tying Laos to Yunnan Province could only diminish Vietnamese influence. The Politburo purge helped reassure Vietnam that Laos was still its kindred spirit.

Somsavat's willingness to put aside politics in the interest   39
of getting something built reflects a very Chinese way of
thinking. But in the end, Laos wasn't ready for this kind of
post-political mindset. For Somsavat, the turnabout must have
been jarring. Forty years earlier, not far from the convention
center, he had stood in a high school gymnasium with victorious
Pathet Lao rebels, drawing up plans for the communist government that had now ejected him. His exit was depicted with
the utmost grace by the state-controlled press—officially, he
simply "didn't stand for re-election"—suggesting that the party's enthusiasm for the railway remains very much alive. Somsavat is even still tangentially involved in its execution, acting
as an unofficial go-between with China, like a retired American
politician taking a job as a lobbyist.

At this point, however, Somsavat may no longer be key
to the project's success. Since his departure, in fact, work on
the ground has accelerated noticeably. Three months after he
stepped down, on April 23, 2016, Chinese Foreign Minister
Wang Yi arrived in Laos eager to discuss progress on the railway.
At that point, there hadn't been much, and Wang Yi was there
to express his disappointment. His conversation with Kham-
khanh Chamthavisouk, the Governor of Laos's Luang Prabang
province, was cordial but tense. Wang Yi reminded the governor that "China and Laos are a community of common des-
tiny. The two countries are strategic partners and the two
peoples are brothers and sisters." For that reason, Wang Yi said
in regard to the still-unbuilt railway, "China has achieved some

40   development in these years, and as a good neighbor, it hopes that Laos will also develop more quickly."

Such icy beads of encouragement continued to drip from Beijing until, on Christmas Day of 2016, Vientiane held a second groundbreaking, nearly a year after the first. The country's new prime minister, Thongloun Sisoulith, stood by as Laos's Minister of Public Works and Transport addressed the crowd. Somsavat stood quietly off to the side. "Once completed, the railway will benefit Lao people of all ethnic groups," said the minister. A Chinese delegate took to the podium to reassure everyone that in the time since the first groundbreaking, engineering had continued apace.

That much appears to be true. By the summer of 2017, Chinese workers were tunneling through the hills around Vang Vieng, a small city north of Vientiane. Around Luang Prabang, workers are clearing the land. In Oudomxay Province, just south of the Lao-Chinese border, villas are reportedly being constructed to house Chinese workers. Suddenly, uncharacteristically, there is a sense that something big is coming to Laos.

To get a glimpse, in March 2017 I took an overnight train from Bangkok to that dusty field near Vientiane, riding in a luxurious new first-class Chinese-built sleeper car. It was the first new rolling stock that State Railways of Thailand had purchased in twenty years. My phone charged in a bedside USB port while a touch-screen TV glowed just beyond my feet. When I reached the Lao capital, I hired a driver and continued north to the city of Boten, a two-day, 400-mile climb over

endless mountain switchbacks. I wanted to see what was going   41
on in the thinly settled China-Laos border region, where work
had finally begun on a railway that had been an imperial fan-
tasy for a hundred years.

A Most Internationally Modernized City

Some sixty miles south of the Chinese border lies Oudomxay, a gritty staging site in northern Laos for heavy industry and a transport hub for regional cargo flows. Twenty years ago this was a highland village, but its population has ballooned to about 25,000 as Chinese entrepreneurs have settled in. Now it's filled with auto dealerships selling steam shovels and street vendors hawking sheet metal. In one shop, I watched an elderly man puff on a PVC pipe that had been turned into a bong. The Sheng Chang Hotel, a six-story palace of purple and gold that's the only glamour to be found in Oudomxay, is largely empty, and the darkened floors above are lit only by glowing blue doorbells that line the halls like runway lights. The hotel's only apparent staff, a Lao receptionist, says the few guests they receive are Chinese project managers, but that they expect to be fully booked before long: Oudomxay will soon have a railway station.

The Sheng Chang sits on one side of the Nam Ko River, which runs along the western edge of town and nourishes a collection of rice paddies that stretches toward the horizon. One of these paddies belongs to Somphone Phomexay, a soft-spoken hydroelectric engineer who was sent to Oudomxay from Vientiane in the 1990s to help build the nearby Nam Ko River Dam. He's worked at the dam ever since, while harvesting rice and fruit trees to supplement his income.

One day in the late summer of 2016, Somphone's village chief asked him and seven of his neighbors to come to a meeting with a poker-faced government official. "The chief explained that our fields would be reclaimed as the site of the railway station," says Somphone. "Then the official helped me fill out an application for compensation." Somphone dutifully filled out the paperwork and handed it over. Shortly thereafter, a team of Chinese surveyors were trundling through his rice paddy, measuring the land.

Somphone's field is part of a rare spit of level land in a province besieged by craggy mountains and misty valleys. It's some of the most rugged terrain on earth, and the railway will run straight through it. An elevation diagram of the route resembles a cardiac patient's heart rate, zigzagging up and down through Northern Laos before flatlining along the plains in the south. The route will require over 150 bridges and 70 tunnels. Seven of these tunnels will be more than four miles long. The mountains are unstable limestone and the area the railway will run through is littered with unexploded ordinance left over from the 270 million bombs dropped on Laos by the U.S. during the Vietnam War. It's enough to cast doubt on whether it will ever be built.

44   And yet, signs of something coming are apparent. Earth-movers sit atop tracts of freshly leveled land all along the roadside from the border to Oudomxay. Chinese workers in blue and white uniforms squat and smoke by aluminum-clad roadside dormitories, their facades sporting royal blue banners marketing the project in Lao and Mandarin: *China Railway Number 5 Engineering Group, Boten-Vientiane Railway Section, Department of Construction Management. Number 1 Concrete Mixing Plant Welcomes You. Building the Laos-China Railway. Bringing Benefits to the Lao and Chinese People.*

Some of the laborers living in these dorms will presumably work at the new cement plant further up the road, just outside the village of Nam Veun. Blue and white silos tower over a billboard celebrating the plant's inauguration, and you can find similar silos downstream from Oudomxay, where the energy company ChinaPower is building a large hydroelectric dam. It's the latest in a string of dams China has constructed on the upper Mekong River. Since the Lao government opened the power sector to foreign investment in 1993, hydroelectricity has become one of Laos's primary exports.

Everything related to the railway, from the cement plants to the workers' jumpsuits, is branded with the same blue and white color scheme and emblazoned with Mandarin characters. It sets them far apart from the rest of the town, visually and geographically. The Chinese generally "prefer to live together in their own circle and are not so sociable with their fellow local employees," as a 2012 memo put out by the Chinese embassy in Nairobi bluntly stated.

On the way to Boten we took a wrong turn—not easy to do in a country with so few roads, but we managed. We ended up in a threadbare village called Nateuy. A group of women was sitting on the side of the road and we stopped to ask directions. They were getting plastered on domestic beer in the early afternoon sun. When I told them why I was in Laos, they groaned in unison. The Chinese were everywhere now, and rude, they said. One of them had even opened a small restaurant without talking to the local village chief first, which the women took as a sign of disrespect. "They just do what they want because they have power," said one of them, wielding her beer. "They just come here and make money."

We stopped at the restaurant they'd complained about. The proprietor ushered us past a row of glass jugs filled with roots and dead turtles floating in clear liquid. We were the only customers, but she seemed impatient for us to order. Photographs of meals were posted on the walls, and she led me by the elbow from photo to photo as if in a gallery. Spicy mapo tofu and rice arrived quickly, and she stared as we ate. It was not at all like the experience of eating at a Lao-owned establishment, a lazy affair of chit-chat and pleasantries. I could see how the rift in cultural norms would leave the Lao feeling disrespected.

A half-abandoned former casino town in the Lao jungle is not where Callan Cheng imagined he'd be living at twenty-nine. Yet here he was in Boten, huddled beneath an umbrella, exiting the shopperless duty-free mall, where he worked as a buyer in a nondescript office high above the aisles of perfume and whiskey.

46   It had been raining for a week straight, and though his apartment building was only a five-minute walk from his office, the
slog from work to home through the muddy streets was a daily
depressant.

At least Cheng lived on the fifth floor. The first and second
floor flats devolved into moldy, moisture-locked terrar-
iums when it rained for days on end like this. He even had his
own room—one of the rare perks of middle management—a
budget-motel motif of hard-tile flooring, bare walls, and shiny
lacquered decor. He'd been living here since 2014, when he was
hired by the Boten Economic Zone Development and Construction Group, a Chinese company headquartered in Kunming. From there, Cheng's company manages the city of Boten
remotely. "We control all of Boten, the entire city," he says. In
effect, the company is the municipal government, adminis-
tering Boten's taxes and finances, public utilities, telecommunications infrastructure, sanitation, emergency services,
its hotels, markets and, of course, the duty-free mall. Likewise, nearly everyone working in Boten is on the company payroll. The Lao public sector has minimal involvement. "They've
authorized us to take care of things," says Cheng.

When the border crossing was established in Boten in 1993,
this region was a thinly settled *terra nullius* of scattered, isolated
mountain settlements. In the early 2000s, the arrival of the
casinos turned the city into a braying haunted carnival, but with
the focus on illicit fun it didn't really develop as a trade hub.
In 2009, a paltry $20 million in Sino-Thai commerce moved
through here. A diplomatic cable from that period described it

as a "remarkably quiet border crossing . . . with one truck and
one bus coming into China" over the course of half an hour.

A decade later, with boring machines slicing a new railway tunnel across the border and trade between China and ASEAN approaching half a trillion dollars per year, Boten is reincarnating, bit by bit, as a commercial hub—a transport link for China into Southeast Asia, and a One Belt One Road priority holding. You can see offshoots of the city's new relevance in the wilderness just beyond its borders, where flashes of alien modernity have materialized: PetroLao gas stations, stucco guesthouses, and the weirdest: a palatial furniture showroom fully stocked with flashy bedroom sets. Sections of the forest have been clear-cut to make way for muddy parking lots filled with flatbed trucks.

At the entrance to Boten is a customs checkpoint, confirmation that you're exiting Laos without actually leaving. Beyond the checkpoint, the jungle torpor immediately evaporates, replaced by a grinding, gridlocked sea of long-haul trucks fighting their way toward the Chinese border. The queue of traffic bypasses Boten's mostly empty core. From afar, in the midday haze, Boten's pastel skyline could pass for a faded Florida resort town. Up close, it looks like what it is: a city slowly regenerating after a population crash.

Around town, some of the former enterprises have been revived. Cheng's cavernous duty-free mall, once a disco, contains Marlboros and Johnnie Walker, but virtually no customers. Young Chinese clerks in sharp black suits wander the quiet aisles like docents in a pop art museum.

48   Down the street, at the Royal Jingland Hotel, the courtyard fountain is filled with muck, and overgrown tropical gardens are climbing the building's exterior walls. A rusting Yamaha motorbike lies in a weedy flowerbed, and one of the electric trams formerly used to shuttle guests around town rusts out on four flat tires. In the lobby, the air is cool and moist. There's a chunk missing from the hotel's back wall, and the gaping hole frames the forest beyond like a diorama of prehistoric life. Most of the rooms are sealed, but a few have been broken into, including one with rumpled bedding on the mattress and the remnants of a nonpaying guest's recently eaten meal. In a third-floor solarium, damp shirts dangle from hangers on a ceiling pipe, drying in the sun. A ransacked supervisor's office is strewn with the minutiae of hotel management: employee schedules, reports typed up in Mandarin, and a Chinese-English dictionary opened on the desk, as if its owner looked up a word, left the room, and never returned.

One of Boten's few hotspots is in the former Golden Casino, readapted as a luminous jade emporium buzzing with a deal-seeking Chinese clientele. A security guard hesitates to admit the unshaven Westerner in the dirty black t-shirt, but a young shopgirl bounds to my rescue: Wang Tingting from Yunnan Province. She strides toward me, arm outstretched, grinning like an old friend. Where do I come from? New York! How exciting! What am I doing in Boten? A book! Interesting! She spirits me inside, muttering something in Mandarin to the guard as we enter before turning to me and playfully rolling her eyes as if to say, "Can you believe that guy?"

With the polished affability of a corporate publicist, Wang whisks me through the marketplace. Thousands of bracelets, necklaces, rings, and amulets glint beneath LED lights, all of them carved from jade mined in Myanmar's conflict-riven Kachin State. "Only the best minerals," Wang assures me, "and something for every ability to pay."

Wang has a wanderer's soul. In her early twenties she moved to Thailand, fell in love with the country, and ended up spending several years there. "I speak Thai, and I want to go back and use it," she says. Six months prior to our meeting she had moved to Boten, hoping to cash in on the boom she believes will inevitably arrive with the high-speed railway. Getting the go-ahead to work in Boten wasn't hard, she says, thanks to the cross-border cooperation pact that expedites permissions for Chinese nationals who want to work here.

The ease with which Wang got the job in Laos is exactly the point of a special economic zone: to eliminate the red tape that delays getting down to business. SEZs chiefly serve as a mechanism for streamlining investment. But as Wang Tingting proves, even a humble store clerk can leverage the perks of an SEZ. "Once the railway is built, this will be an important place to work," she informs me.

Cheng agrees that those willing to spend a few years here will eventually be rewarded. "I don't like living in Boten," he says. "It's too deserted for me." He hopes to someday return to the cacophonous clang of Kunming, where he was raised an only child in the modern Chinese tradition. Or better yet, glitzy Shanghai, his city of dreams. For now, however, he's biding his

50   time. "I think in five years, Boten will be a big city," says Cheng. "Not huge, but better than now. I think there will be over 100,000 people, tourists, people doing business. It's the first station on the railway for Chinese people going to ASEAN, so it will be important for logistics. I want to have a chance to be part of its development."

In the city center, this development is beginning to take shape. A trio of poured-concrete towers, the fledgling skyline of the renovated Boten, rise amid a tangle of cranes. According to Cheng, the redevelopment plan calls for a total of six downtown buildings that will constitute some form of miniature central business district. Some of these buildings can be seen in renderings posted at the construction site: The tawdry sin city has vanished, replaced by a bright, wholesome streetscape of boulevards and cafés.

Boten is sketched as originally sold: a most internationally modernized city, now in development by a Chinese consortium under a reported ninety-nine-year concession. "The anarchy of the border country is, for those with capital and connections and the ability to exploit it, a giant opportunity," writes Ben Rawlence in the book *City of Thorns*. For Boten's new opportunists, the fledgling logistics hub promises this and more: the chance to cash in on a massive global trade initiative at one of its most promising frontiers.

That frontier's future is depicted on glossy flyers stacked by the unmanned cash registers at the duty-free mall, with renderings of the new-and-improved Boten, a happy city with a high-speed train. In the center of the flyers is a photo of

President Xi, and below him, a map of the world. Dotted lines
lead outward from China to points throughout Asia, Europe, and
Africa. The cities key to making One Belt One Road a success
are marked with stars: Singapore, Mombasa, Tehran, Colombo,
Moscow, Rotterdam, and a tiny city in northern Laos, perfectly
placed on the route of a high-speed railway, its location labeled
in Mandarin and marked with the biggest star of them all.

Win-Win

China wants the world to love it, which often starts with convincing countries that China isn't scary. It's been a tough sell, and by one estimate the country spends $10 billion per year on its soft power programs. To this end, Beijing has set up hundreds of Confucius Institutes around the world to teach foreigners Chinese language and history, and promoted its Xinhua news agency throughout the West.

But all the spending has failed to endear the world to the Chinese way. Chinese soft power is tainted by the regime's own authoritarianism and reputation for narrative control. In 2016, an electronic billboard in New York's Times Square played a video defending China's claims in the South China Sea using jaunty music and images of inviting azure water and tropical isles. Chinese media reported the video "appealed to a massive number of people," but in reality, it was widely

ridiculed as a ham-handed article of propaganda. This is Beijing's conundrum.

So China has turned to its unparalleled knack for construction as its soft power tactic of choice. Like the United States,
China today frames its foreign priorities as a force for global
good. All development is said to be "win-win," and evidence
to the contrary won't debunk this hypothesis. But while China's message echoes the West's, its methods of development are
notably different, a reality the countries touched by One Belt
One Road are just beginning to settle into. In return for helping
poorer countries modernize, China often expects to be granted
de facto control over a piece of those countries. Not to colonize
that piece—simply to monetize it. Not to own it, per se, but to
access and utilize it in a way that benefits China directly.

Boten Golden City and the high-speed railway are very different projects, but they're similar in one respect: They're local-
ized transfers of governmental control from one country to
another. Within the perimeters of these sites, Laos, to varying
degrees, has relinquished its national sovereignty in exchange
for modernization, giving China jurisdiction over a substantial
amount of its land.

When China turned Boten into a mini Macau, it was on the
cusp of surpassing Germany as the world's top exporter. Economic growth was humming along at an annual average of 11
percent. An unusually large workforce and the economic fore-
sight of Deng Xiaoping, China's paramount leader from 1978 to
1989, was to thank, but so were Beijing's weighty investments

54   in the country's now famous infrastructure projects. By 2010, the Chinese government was spending roughly half of its GDP on these types of investments, a greater share than any other country had ever spent before.

The spending spree gave China the mantle of the most prolific builder the world had ever seen, but also more factories, airports, and apartment buildings than it really needs. Overbuilt at home, China started looking for other places to pour its concrete; this desire to offload excess capacity is one of the motivations for the One Belt One Road initiative. It's also why China has begun building trains and railways for other countries, working to position itself as the world's go-to general contractor for all things rail.

China considers this "railway diplomacy," a strategy formally launched in 2011 to sell Chinese rail hardware and technology to transport ministries around the world. Premier Li Keqiang is the effort's foremost pitchman, hopscotching from Romania to India, talking up Chinese high-speed trains as a transit solution and an economic boon. He travels with a shiny model train, the porpoise-nosed CRH380A, a Chinese design that Japan has complained is a knockoff of its iconic Shinkansen. He traveled to Addis Ababa in 2014, after which the African Union signed an action plan to connect every major city in Africa to high-speed rail by 2063. He went to Brazil in May 2015 to convince then-President Dilma Rousseff of the need to cut a transcontinental railway through the Amazon rainforest. By that point, China was in talks with nearly thirty countries about high-speed rail projects, with plans to double its overseas rail contracts by the year 2020.

All this pitching has occurred amid China's rise to the summit of the world's rail industry. By 2015, 41 percent of global rail revenues were flowing to Chinese companies. That same year, China merged its two state-owned railcar manufacturers to create the second-largest industrial company after GE, the China Railway Rolling Stock Corporation (CRRC). It began peddling its trains everywhere, including, for the first time, in the United States, starting with a $566 million contract with the Massachusetts transit authority, the MBTA.

Before China came in, the chronically cash-strapped MBTA was simply going to rehab its old subway cars, some of which had been creaking along for 46 years. But CRRC's bid for the project— over $100 million lower than the closest competitor's—made it more financially sensible for the agency to purchase new cars from China than to spruce up the old ones. The MBTA ordered 284 subway cars for its red and orange lines, and in April 2017, a two-thirds size mockup was unveiled at City Hall Plaza. Shipped from Beijing's Tianjin Port and wrapped in a giant orange bow, gone was the disco-era wood paneling and worn, bacteria-absorbent upholstery. Through an interpreter, CRRC representative An Zhongyi thanked the crowd for "believing in our ability to lead this project," while a crop-topped subway busker named Vivian Luo played her violin. The new cars would allow the MBTA to cut intervals between trains to as little as three minutes, increasing the overwhelmed system's capacity by 10,000 passengers per hour.

China's leap into the U.S. railway market was a game-changer for American cities accustomed to scraping by with trains from the 1970s. Massachusetts rushed through a second order with CRRC for another 134 cars because, as the state's transportation secretary put it, "We want them to do ours, and we don't want them to do someone else's."

But CRRC was already doing someone else's. It signed contracts with Philadelphia and Los Angeles, and struck a deal to replace half of Chicago's fleet—its biggest order ever from a developed country. A few local pols scored points with the requisite grumblings about Chinese encroachment, but the truth was, no American company had been competitive on the global passenger railcar market in years, and in any case, CRRC was building or investing in U.S.-based factories where hardworking Americans, some of them trained in China, would assemble the trains themselves. For these transit agencies, China was more of a savior than a threat, enabling them to update their systems with state-of-the-art technology at a price point they'd never seen.

This everybody-wins dynamic is exactly how China wants the world to see its rail diplomacy, and by extension, the sprawling One Belt One Road initiative as a whole. "Now that China has developed, it is our turn to contribute," is how the head of China's Asian Infrastructure Investment Bank magnanimously put it in a 2017 interview. Railways, highways, airports—these are public goods. They drive growth and improve real people's lives, and China hopes to be known as the world's friendly neighborhood builder of them. In 2014, China's outbound investment flows surged past $100 billion, up 14 percent from the year before. And the money didn't only go to middle-income countries. It tripled its investments in the

European Union and boosted its spending in the U.S. by 24 percent. All told, 156 countries and regions received Chinese investment that year.

Though this scope is unprecedented, diplomacy via infrastructure has been a Chinese diplomatic tactic for decades. In the early 1970s, Mao Zedong, estranged from both the Soviets and the West, built the TAZARA Railway for Tanzania and Zambia to shore up Chinese ties to Africa. He picked an opportune moment to do so. Institutions like the World Bank were broadening their focus to include social welfare rubrics like health and education. China, meanwhile, began exporting infrastructure, more to make friends than money. Even then, the Chairman framed the TAZARA project as a gift from one struggling nation to another. "You have difficulties as we do," Mao told the leaders of both countries. "To help you build the railway, we are willing to forsake building railways for ourselves."

Three decades later, when an ascendant Beijing hosted the 2008 Summer Games, it started the torch relay's Africa run at the TAZARA train station in Dar es Salaam. The symbolism was potent. It had been thirty-three years since China built the terminal, back when it and Tanzania were third-world brethren barely scratching by. Now China was the world's eclipsing superpower and still building megaprojects for its African friend, which still languishes in the lower-income country bracket. The torch relay literally traced the path of China's investment in Tanzania, ending at the National Stadium built with Chinese money in 2007. It was a tribute, but also a reminder—a public tallying of the "historical evidence of China's selfless help to

58   Africa," as a white paper issued by the State Council in Beijing tactfully put it.

Today, China is laying more tracks than ever across East Africa. When the Chinese-built Nairobi-Mombasa train made its inaugural run on May 31, 2017—a year ahead of schedule—clouds of confetti swirled in the breeze. President Uhuru Kenyatta bluntly distinguished the project from the colonial railways that came before it, specifically the British-built, derailment-prone "Lunatic Express." "We now celebrate not the Lunatic Express, but the Madaraka Express," Kenyatta said proudly, "that will begin to reshape the story of Kenya for the next hundred years."

But scarcely had the words left his mouth that analysts were debating the railway's consequences. Would it reshape Kenya's future, as Kenyatta promised, or capsize its economy? Governments on the receiving end of railway diplomacy sometimes find that their new "partnership" with China has instantly made the People's Republic their biggest creditor. The Madaraka Express was built with a $3.8 billion loan from China's Export-Import Bank that nudged Kenya's debt above half of its GDP. This is why the World Bank declined to finance the project in 2013, concluding there was no "economic or financial case" for a standard-gauge railway from the capital city to the coast.

Of course, this is the same World Bank that argued against building a Shanghai subway in 1991. But with national balance sheets at stake, some healthy skepticism is warranted. The economic and technical challenges of even cut-rate high-speed rail are why, despite its efforts, China still hasn't completed a

high-speed rail project abroad. A Chinese-led high-speed link
connecting Jakarta with Bandung in Indonesia has been mired
in budget and land-acquisition problems since 2015. Deals for
China to build high-speed rail for Mexico, Brazil, and the U.S.
have all collapsed, often because in the end the projects were
deemed not entirely necessary. But China isn't in the business
of determining whether other countries really need high-speed
rail, it's in the business of selling those countries high-speed
rail regardless. In January 2017, Fitch Ratings released a report
warning that some aspects of One Belt One Road "might not be
aimed at addressing the most pressing infrastructure needs,"
but instead at "China's efforts to extend its global influence and
relieve domestic overcapacity."

That much should be obvious. Despite China's claim that
it is simply "our turn to contribute," One Belt One Road is a
high-stakes geopolitical game plan to augment and fortify Chinese power. A press release from the State Council of China notes
with clarity that "high-speed rail is a strategy rather than just a
normal project." By their very nature, strategic projects aren't
necessarily designed to turn a profit—they may be written off
as loss leaders in service of a longer-term goal. For China, these
losses are baked into the budget. But for the poorer countries
partnering with China to build them, the debt amassed when
big dreams become white elephants can be ruinous.

Take the case of Sri Lanka. Recently emerged from a grinding
civil war, the island nation is desperate for infrastructure and
China has been more than happy to lend a hand. It loaned the
Sri Lankan government $300 million for a seaport and built a

flashy new airport nearby. But the interest rate for the seaport loan was a sharkbite 6.3 percent, and the airport is so underutilized that guards were reportedly hired to prevent local wildlife from turning the empty concourse into an indoor habitat.

The deal and others like it left Sri Lanka owing China $8 billion it couldn't repay. When the Chinese Foreign Ministry addressed this debt at a press gaggle in March 2015, one could detect a thinly veiled threat when the spokesperson advised Sri Lanka to "properly resolve relevant problems . . . in the overall interests of China-Sri Lanka friendliness." And so, financially hogtied, Sri Lanka agreed to give Beijing an 80 percent stake in the seaport China had just "contributed" to Sri Lanka's shores in exchange for forgiving some of its debt. This stake was reduced after public protests, but the outcome remained the same: Beijing got control of one of the most strategically placed deep-sea ports in the world. The result of a deal supposedly gone wrong for China was another pin in the Belt and Road map, floating directly in the path of the shipping lanes linking Asia, Africa, and the Middle East.

Did China intend for the Sri Lankan loan deal to self-destruct as a way of acquiring control of the port? To better understand Beijing's motives, I met with Parag Khanna in Singapore. Khanna's bio describes him as a "global strategist." His resumé is a gravitas salad of special advisory credits, think-tank fellowships, best-selling books, board affiliations, and advanced degrees. But in person he's loose, even goofy. He suggested we meet at Atlas, an extravagant faux art deco bar in downtown Singapore, to which

he arrived in shorts and flipflops in cheerful defiance of the
dress code. Wolfing grilled octopus and throwing his leg over
the arm of his leather chair, he notes that while the previous
Sri Lankan government had been friendly with China, the current one had been stubbornly resistant to Beijing's overtures.
But after the port deal went south, "Sri Lanka's debt exposure
to China was so high, they had no choice but to go back to the
pro-China stance of the government before them," says Khanna.
"That's crafty planning."

"I have an equation I use to measure how fucked your
country is in its relationship with China," he says. It's a back-
of-the-napkin appraisal designed to make a point. "Your numer-
ator is your debt to China, and your denominator is your total
outstanding debt. The result is the share of your country's debt
owed to China." The higher the number, the more you're "fucked."

Loans from China comprise about $8 billion of Sri Lanka's
total $65 billion national debt. "A number of countries fall into
my little mathematical formula," says Khanna. "And that's by
design. China leverages this debt to get other things it wants.
Oh, you just defaulted on your payment? Okay, you have to sell
us your next oil and gas exploration concession at a fire sale
price. Or your next tranche of sovereign debt issuance will be in
renminbi instead of dollars."

Proponents of this theory have labeled it "debt-trap diplomacy," with one scholar alleging that "China is taking steps to
ensure that countries will not be able to escape their debts."
Sri Lanka isn't the first country to be backed against a wall
by Chinese generosity. Just a tick northwest, the $55 billion

62   China-Pakistan Economic Corridor (CPEC), a web of roads, rail, and energy infrastructure linking China to the Arabian Sea, threatens to beckon Pakistan onto similarly thin fiscal ice. One of Pakistan's former finance ministers estimates that CPEC loans could raise the country's debt level by $14 billion, bringing it to a total of $90 billion. A BMI Research report warned that this could put Pakistan in a position "similar to the situation that Sri Lanka currently finds itself in." Already, the deal has secured China a forty-year lease on Gwadar Port, a supremely strategic location for any country hoping to secure its interests in the Persian Gulf.

To Khanna, if China is indeed burdening countries with debt they can't afford, that's simply savvy mercantilism. "It's not China's fault its neighbors are poor and backward and badly governed and need infrastructure," he says. "China itself was that country forty years ago. The only way for China to get things done is to indebt them further." As for China's feel-good assertion that it is simply its turn to contribute, Khanna laughs. "There's no such thing as a benevolent empire." Crafty and charitable don't really mix.

And yet, for the city of Springfield, the MBTA's new $95 million, 204,000-square-foot railcar factory certainly feels like a blend of both. To be sure, that plant is a straightforward business venture, not a strategic attempt to indebt the state of Massachusetts. But it stands as an example of Beijing's win-win sloganeering playing out in real life. China opened the facility on the site of the city's former Westinghouse Electric plant, 125 years after Springfield manufactured one of the United

States's first gas-powered cars. It's the biggest industrial venture in decades to arrive in the post-manufacturing city, which
slowly rusted out alongside the Buffalos and Detroits in the late
twentieth century. In April 2017, as thirty-three union sheet
metal workers, engineers, and supervisors boarded a flight—
the first of three on their thirty-hour journey to Jilin Province
for training—Springfield's mayor referred to them as workforce
pioneers. "It's back to the future with establishing manufacturing in Springfield," he told the China-bound workers, "and
you are a big part of that."

In the actual *Back to the Future* trilogy, the "future" Marty
McFly works for a Japanese company in 2015. (His boss, Mr.
Fujitsu, fires him by fax.) That movie, the second in the series,
was released in 1989, when Hollywood fashionably assumed
that your average American would someday be working for
Mr. Fujitsu. And although that future never came to pass, it's
tempting, three decades later, to look at blue-collar laborers
flying off to work for a Chinese company as equally predestined.

But China's resurgence was never a lock. Other developing countries with plenty of cheap labor and resources have
grown more slowly, and China's infrastructure binge alone
can't explain the gap. China emerged from its treacherous
Maoist period with a relatively large, healthy, literate workforce for such a poor country. Deng Xiaoping leveraged this
shovel-ready citizenry by declaring China open for business
just as the rise of globalization demanded a factory to the
world. Now, with the U.S. pivoting inward, China is eager to

64   level-up once again as the dominant force in Asia, a key priority for President Xi.

Since coming to power, Xi has moved China away from
the dictum that it focus chiefly on strengthening its economy
at home and worked to create a Chinese sphere of influence
through what Tom Miller, author of *China's Asian Dream*, calls "a
web of informal alliances lubricated by Chinese cash." At base,
these alliances are economic, but they're also strategic, to the
point that the One Belt One Road initiative has become virtually
inseparable from Chinese foreign policy. "Beijing is not seeking
to build a formal alliance structure," writes Miller. Instead, it's
pursuing a range of mutually beneficial geostrategic partnerships buttressed by development and trade.

Despite claims of a "peaceful rise," these One Belt One
Road partnerships could come in handy down the line as China
increasingly asserts itself as a regional power. Its most visible
posturing occurs in the South China Sea, but its presence can
be felt around the Indian Ocean, in Sri Lanka, Pakistan, down
the Southeast Asian peninsula, and beyond. Some experts have
theorized that with these seaports, airfields, and industrial
zones, China is strategically lacing a "string of pearls" along the
rim of the Indian Ocean that can one day act as a naval strong-
hold to complement—and protect—its commercial interests.
So far, however, there's no smoking gun to prove this theory.

But even without such naval bases installed, China is
already reaping geostrategic benefits from its economic "partnerships" with other countries. A prime example is Malaysia,
a major recipient of Chinese investment. Malaysia and China

have overlapping territorial claims to islands in the South China
Sea. But compared to countries like Vietnam and the Philip-
pines, the Malaysian government has been relatively muted in
its grievances, saying the dispute should be resolved as a civil
discussion between friends. That's probably smart, given that
China has become one of Malaysia's biggest sources of foreign
investment, not to mention its largest trading partner since
2009, with bilateral trade between the two countries topping
$50 billion in 2016. Malaysia's fiscal ledgers also happen to be
awash in red ink these days. If China were to back out of some
of its major investments, that would leave Malaysia, its "good
partner and good neighbor," as Beijing likes to call it, in a pretty
inconvenient spot.

Good Partners and Good Neighbors

On a 486-acre site on Kuala Lumpur's southern periphery, Malaysia is preparing to construct a new neighborhood anchored by a high-speed railway terminal. The master-planned, mixed-use district will be built atop the tarmacs of the city's decommissioned international airport, more recently used as a base by the Royal Malaysian Air Force. Renderings of the proposed development show the familiar infinite-city aesthetic of Southeast Asian urbanism: glass skyscrapers, shopping malls, an artificial lake ringed with greenery. Touted as "the catalyst for the transformation of greater Kuala Lumpur," Bandar Malaysia, as the new district will be known, amounts to a vast expansion of the capital, to be built from the ground up.

The original concept for Bandar Malaysia, which began taking shape in 2011, had transit lines connecting it to the rest of Kuala Lumpur, but no high-speed railway terminal. It wasn't until 2013 that the governments of Malaysia and Singapore approved a project to link their two countries with a high-speed train. (Singapore will build a similar district around its own terminal.) At a signing ceremony on December 13, 2016, Singaporean Prime Minister Lee Hsien Loong and Malaysian Prime Minister Najib Razak formally launched the project. The 217-mile Kuala Lumpur-Singapore High-Speed Railway (KLSR) will bisect Malaysia's densely settled west coast, providing a ninety-minute alternative to the current four-hour drive between the two cities.

The addition of the train attracted China's attention. Bandar was no longer simply a "creative enterprise hub," as its promotional materials describe it, but an opportunity to add another transport link to the One Belt One Road map. Conceived and planned entirely by the governments of Malaysia and Singapore, the KLSR is not a China-propelled project like the railway in Laos. But China sees it as advancing its expansion objectives in Southeast Asia regardless. Chinese officials often mention the railway in the same breath as the larger One Belt One Road initiative, and hope its construction could entice Thailand to build tracks southward to Kuala Lumpur, bringing a contiguous route from Kunming to Singapore another step closer to reality.

At the very least, the KLSR presents an opportunity for railway diplomacy—Singapore and Malaysia are seeking a builder for the railway, and China has bid aggressively for the contract. China's chief rival in this regard is Japan, home of the world's first bullet train, which is also vying for the contract for the project, worth up to $18 billion. Wealthy Singapore was said to favor working with Japan, while Malaysia was leaning toward China, which had already secured the contract

68   for another Malaysian rail link connecting the country's east and west coasts.

Japan has repeatedly sent delegates to Kuala Lumpur to make a characteristically Japanese pitch, emphasizing its reputation for precision craftsmanship and safety, the high-class alternative to China's cut-rate construction. The high-speed train wreck that killed 40 people in the suburb of Wenzhou—the result, in part, of a rushed construction schedule—still haunts China's rail-building reputation. And yet, during China's own pitch to Malaysian officials, a Chinese envoy embraced his country's usual sales pitch, insisting to a reporter that the KLSR's "construction timeframe of ten years is too long. Five years would be enough."

Chinese officials also deployed their go-to tactic of constantly reminding Malaysia's leaders of their countries' "friendly relations" as "good partners and good neighbors." The neighborliness dates to 1974 when Malaysia, then run by Najib's father, became the first ASEAN country to establish diplomatic ties with communist China. In recent years, the two nations have grown even closer. In 2015, China decided to locate its first overseas railcar factory in Malaysia's Perak State. Nearly half the value of all foreign construction projects in Malaysia was provided by China in 2015. President Xi has characterized his relationship with Najib as the "best ever."

This goodwill groundwork set the stage for one of China's biggest gestures yet, one that would instantly reconfigure the race for the KLSR contract. In December 2015, China Railway Engineering Corp. (CREC), partnering with a Malaysia-based real estate developer, agreed to buy a 60 percent stake in Bandar Malaysia for $1.7 billion. In fact, not only would CREC buy into the massive real estate development, it would pour another $2 billion into the property to establish its Southeast Asian headquarters there.

For Malaysians leery of Chinese saturation, the news went off like an air raid siren. "Bandar Malaysia Has Become Bandar China," blared the headline atop one blog. In one fell swoop, Malaysia had abdicated control of its biggest real estate venture to a foreign power and launched that power to the top of its foreign investor list. The government insisted that because the buying consortium included a Malaysia-based developer, Bandar Malaysia was still technically a majority-Malaysian holding. But the simpler story stuck: China, having eclipsed Singapore as Malaysia's top trading partner in 2009, had outstripped the island city-state as the biggest investor in Malaysian property, too.

In a country where resentment of Chinese wealth simmers just below the surface, the optics of the deal would have ruffled feathers under these circumstances alone. But the alleged motive for the sale was salt in the wound. At the time, Najib's administration was being hammered in the press for a political scandal that stemmed from 1MDB, a state-owned investment fund put in place by Najib in 2009 to fund a range of economic development projects to boost the Malaysian economy. But according to investigators, 1MDB became little more than a box of petty cash that associates of the prime minister could dip into to fund their wildest dreams. Upward of $4 billion was

70 allegedly misappropriated to people who blew it on everything from corporate jets to lavish Los Angeles mansions. The Swiss attorney general called it a ponzi scheme.

By the middle of 2016, 1MDB was the subject of a U.S. Department of Justice lawsuit, the target of multiple investigations across several countries, and according to the U.S. attorney general, the "largest kleptocracy case" in American history. Najib himself was accused of receiving nearly $700 million, a charge he denied. Through an asset liquidation program, the government raced to draw down 1MDB's enormous debt. The sell-off of Bandar Malaysia was a crucial part of this effort.

The Bandar deal was a lifeline for a prime minister drowning in red ink, bad press, and litigation. The *Straits Times* went right ahead and branded the sale a Chinese "bailout," but whether it was a well-timed gift or a prudent investment was beside the point. Either way, it had the effect of infusing the KLSR with the glow of Chinese generosity. Suddenly the idea of awarding Japan the contract to build it seemed awfully ungrateful. "We are entering the fight with both hands tied," despaired a Japanese executive.

That all changed on May 3, 2017, however, when Malaysia's Ministry of Finance abruptly called off the deal to sell the Bandar Malaysia stake to the Chinese consortium. In a terse announcement, the ministry declared the agreement dead on arrival and blamed the buyers, claiming the contract was canceled because they had "failed to meet the payment obligations."

The consortium disputed this, countering that it didn't "fully and accurately reflect the circumstances." But the ministry's explanation was accepted by many observers as plausible.

Four months earlier, China's central bank had declared that its foreign exchange reserves had dipped below $3 trillion, an unofficial panic zone. This triggered a series of capital controls that reined in how much renminbi could flow out of the country and into foreign megaprojects. Under the clampdown, a $1.7 billion train station in Kuala Lumpur—with a $2 billion headquarters to come—was the kind of luxury purchase Beijing might choose to postpone.

Others speculated that the land for Bandar had ballooned in value since negotiations began, prompting Malaysia to back out in hopes of finding a better deal. Or perhaps the accusations that he was China's lapdog had finally gotten to Najib, who felt the need to pen a defensive op-ed saying he would "make no apologies for wanting to build world-class infrastructure for Malaysia."

"It's not as if this was a one-shot thing," says Oh Ei Sun, who served as Najib's political secretary from 2009 to 2011. "The location is extremely attractive. If this deal doesn't go through, they can get another buyer, from China or elsewhere." Shortly after the Bandar deal with China collapsed, the Japanese Minister of Land, Infrastructure, Transport, and Tourism was back in Kuala Lumpur and Singapore, talking up Japanese train technology and announcing a fresh push "for a specific proposal involving financing, talent development, and collaboration with local companies."

China could stage a triumphant comeback, returning with a fresh proposal that wins it the contract anew for Bandar Malaysia and for the high-speed railway itself. But if it doesn't,

72 there are other options. "China generally has very vague end goals," says Oh Ei Sun. That's certainly the case with One Belt One Road, the stated aims of which are as nebulous as they are varied: promote connectivity, strengthen trade relations, control supply chains, invest abroad—goals that, by design, can be reached in any number of ways. It's this fluidity that gives some Chinese foreign ventures their hallucinatory surreality: soaring suspension bridges to nowhere and factory towns marooned in the desert.

One of these ventures can be found in the placid waters just off the Malaysian coast, spitting distance from the KLSR's final scheduled stop before it pulls into Singapore. On a string of manmade islands in the Johor Strait, the narrow strip of water that separates Malaysia from Singapore, China is building a city. As of this writing, it's a skyline of half-finished towers wrapped in polyethylene sheeting. Anyone looking to buy a condo is welcome to poke around, so a Singaporean friend and I took a trip across the Johor-Singapore Causeway on a scorching Sunday in May.

As with Boten and Bandar Malaysia, China's city is the product of a twenty-first-century land-use logic in which urbanism can be partially divorced from claims of national territory. By working together to densify Malaysia's southernmost shores, Malaysia and China hope to absorb the thermal energy of adjacent Singapore's economy. Singapore, meanwhile, views the new development as an extension of its own

borders—a guest bedroom that its cramped island residents
can invest in and settle into. It's yet another synergistic,
win-win One Belt One Road special. Singapore will provide
the prosperity, and China is building the city. Malaysia simply
kicked in the land.

A Sanctuary of Utter Peace

Forest City is a Chinese development with room for 700,000 residents being built across a string of manmade islands just off the coast of Malaysia. Since bridges spanning the Johor Strait directly connect Malaysia and Singapore—they were a single entity until 1965—the $100 billion development is marketed chiefly as Singapore-adjacent. Promotional materials call it a "global cluster of commerce and culture," as if it pledges allegiance to no country at all, and note that a new light rail system will connect it to the nearby KLSR.

In the sales showroom, the city's sheer size was on display in its glitzy scale model, which itself was nearly big enough for a child to lumber through like a marauding Godzilla. The model's twisty silver condo towers were strewn with hanging gardens and purple LED lights, lending it a hip moon colony vibe. Several had SOLD OUT signs hanging across their facades.

I rubbernecked my way through three- and four-bedroom model apartments at the heel of a sales associate named Fancy. Fancy was from China's Guangdong Province and outfitted in a retro-trendy *kebaya*. Nothing escaped her laser pen: high-backed armchairs, bejeweled throw pillows, all-clad kitchenware. Floor to ceiling windows overlooked an electric-blue sea. On a living room's wall-mounted TV, a promotional video featured Chinese couples saying things like, "Many ethnic Chinese live here. For us, it's more like we're living in our hometown than a foreign country."

This is Forest City's pitch in a nutshell: Live in China, but in Singapore . . . in Malaysia. As an American business owner working in Southeast Asia told me, "There are a lot of Chinese who don't want to live in China, but they still want to live in 'China.'" Forest City is "like a Chinatown," as one retiree from the gritty factory city of Hangzhou brightly remarked to the *Asia Times*, explaining why she'd purchased a bungalow there.

From the start, Forest City's target market has been residents of places thousands of miles away—congested, smoggy Chinese cities like Tianjin and Guangzhou, where Country Garden, the China-based developer building Forest City, has bought airtime in local media markets and pitched its "near Singapore" condos directly to escapist Chinese buyers.

Malaysia has accommodated inflows of Chinese immigrants in the past. In the middle of the nineteenth century, soldiers fighting in the Crimean War and the American Civil War sent demand for canned foods soaring. Malaysia had some of

76   the world's largest tin deposits, and the country invited Chinese laborers in to excavate its tin mines. By the late 1800s, it was the source of half the global tin supply. Over the years, thousands of these Chinese workers settled in Malaysia permanently, becoming restaurateurs, opium den proprietors, and canning tycoons. Today, Chinese is the second-largest ethnic group in the country, though the government is loathe to grant full citizenship to new arrivals.

Instead, it created the uniquely generous Malaysia My Second Home visa (MM2H), which grants nearly unlimited entry to expats with sufficient disposable income, short of providing citizenship. MM2H has made Malaysia one of the easiest nations on earth to move to. Good for ten years and a breeze to renew, it's effectively a pass for permanent residency. Its main requirements are a bank account with about $120,000 in liquid cash and a monthly offshore income of approximately $2,500, a low bar to clear for a lifelong stay. In 2016, 44 percent of the visa's successful applicants were Chinese.

Forest City is one small part of Iskandar Malaysia, an economic growth corridor that hugs the Malaysian coast just across the water from Singapore. The corridor is roughly modeled on Shenzhen, the celebrated Chinese special economic zone, with a development plan that aims to make it "a strong and sustainable metropolis of international standing" by 2025.

Whether the Shenzhen comparison fits, China has taken a shine to Iskandar, lining its shores with swarms of affordable-luxury condominium towers. If Forest City didn't suit us, Fancy said, might she suggest Danga Bay, an "integrated waterfront living" city up the road, a brisk four miles from the bridge to Singapore. There's also Princess Cove, three times the size of Danga Bay, and a multitude of similar Chinese-built developments in various stages of completion.

It's tempting to smirk at these crystal castles set atop artificial islands in the sea—their bedazzled throw pillows, their nouveau riche names, their brochures promising "a sanctuary of utter peace." But watching hopeful young families poke around the model apartments at Forest City, seeing couples take selfies on the white-sand beach while their kids ran amok in the mist-machine playground, I couldn't help but think that this was an ideal setup for people who were, as the Cathay Pacific in-flight advertisement put it, connecting to One Belt One Road opportunities. If One Belt One Road is an effort to make national borders more permeable, places like Forest City, aided by devices like the MM2H visa, are a credible means to that end—financially feasible living arrangements for a particular brand of Asian expat.

It's a reminder that One Belt One Road, like China's "Go Out" strategy, is a diktat to the Chinese people to barnstorm the world with entrepreneurial ventures and speculative real estate. Ideally, all these molecular enterprises congeal into economic ecosystems, just as America's infrastructural blitz helped happen in Europe seventy years ago. Of the Marshall Plan's many ambitions, high on the list was ensuring that Europe was stable and moneyed enough to siphon off postwar America's residual export glut. Now China has a similar glut, and a similar

78   goal: to urbanize the listless, hazy stretches of soggy farmland that slumber between Southeast Asia's urban cores.

It's not hard to imagine the Forest City template cloned with overhead-shearing efficiency along the railway's route, as those with knowledge of the project believe will happen. Asia has reverse-engineered the art of urbanization, in which entire cities are constructed from scratch and sold unit by unit in air-conditioned sales showrooms.

"The challenge will be, when the high-speed rail arrives in the middle of these places, how do the government planners use it to turn those areas into communities?" says Ed Baker, who led the team of architects that designed Bandar Malaysia. With red marker, he draws a slightly wavy vertical line on a white-board, punctuating it with dots. "Some of these stops on the high-speed rail, the stations are in a *kampong*"—a Malaysian village with stilt-raised clapboard houses topped with roofs of corrugated tin. "It's a village in the romantic sense. People live in little houses with little gardens."

The high-speed rail station for the city of Seremban, for instance, won't be in Seremban proper, but ten miles west in sleepy Labu, a wooded enclave of country roads and palm oil mills. With a high-speed railway station looming, property developers have already reported a rise in land values, where both density and community resistance to development are likely to be low. "You'll find a lot of private developers are interested in these *kampongs*," says Baker. "One might say, 'I'm going to take two thousand hectares and build an office park and I'm going to call it High-Speed City.'"

Mahathir Mohamad, Malaysia's former prime minister, has emerged as the de facto voice of the "Malaysia First" constituency, issuing frequent warnings about all this Chinese-backed development. Armed with an ornery blog, he's been outspoken in his alarm over the idea that "much of the most valuable land will now be owned and occupied by foreigners." In effect, he writes, these developments "will become foreign land."

If Chinese developers are eager to dive in, so are millions of individual Chinese, who see these projects not as steroids for China's state-run economy, but as opportunities for personal gain. Of all the tools for generating wealth, transportation infrastructure is history's favorite. Two centuries ago the State of Georgia stuck a mile marker post in the ground. It became the eastern terminus of the Western and Atlantic Railroad. The city that sprung up around it was originally called Terminus, and is now called Atlanta. It was built by the bricklayers, gas workers, bankers, and machinists who flocked there for a piece of the transit-oriented action.

Today in Southeast Asia, the marbled hotels, dump truck dealerships, mapo tofu joints, and jade emporiums appearing along the railway's route make up the "variety of meso- and mini-projects [that] thrive on the tailwinds of the megaprojects," as the anthropologist Chris Lyttleton calls them. They're the product of millions of Chinese migrants following China-built railways, highways, airports, and seaports into the deserts and jungles, setting up shop as they go.

President Xi has lately been apt to quote a particular Chinese proverb when speaking to provincial leaders and state-linked CEOs: *If you want to get rich, first build a road.* It's not the road itself that offers a return on investment, but the people who choose to follow it. The infrastructure of One Belt One Road, no matter what country it's in, exists, in part, for the *haiwai huaren*—the "overseas Chinese"—syncing their personal life ambitions with Beijing's long-term macroeconomic strategies.

In Forest City, I wondered where all the *haiwai huaren* were. I arrived expecting planeloads of buyers from cities like Wuxi and Nanjing. What I found instead were mostly Malaysian families, the women shielding themselves from the dry-season sun with their hijabs, and sharply dressed Singaporean investors inquiring about subletting policies.

In 2016, Chinese buyers scooped up $33 billion in offshore real estate, a 53 percent increase from the year before. But the same capital controls that may have blasted China out of Bandar Malaysia had strafed the Iskandar waterfront condominium market as well. Panicked about its currency reserves, Beijing instructed Chinese citizens buying real estate abroad to keep their money at home instead, shaking property markets from Auckland to L.A.

Suddenly, future Forest City residents who had already forked over 10 percent down payments were being sent to Hong Kong and Macau to continue paying their installments. As Forest City's sales offices in mainland China closed "for

renovations," new ones began seeking out new clientele in Singapore, Jakarta, and Kuala Lumpur. On the Bank of Shanghai's
mobile app, a pop-up warning cautioned users not to buy foreign exchange if they planned to use it to purchase property
outside of China.

Debate quickly turned to whether Forest City, which had
just handed over the keys to its first 132 apartments, would
become one of China's infamous ghost cities. Meticulously
planned and constructed for a million no-show buyers, these
ghost cities have become irresistible metaphors, cracks in the
dyke for Western audiences eager for proof of Chinese fallibility.

One of the earliest ghost cities to rise to infamy was Ordos
Kangbashi, which broke ground in 2003 on the plateau of Inner
Mongolia, an autonomous region of China. A visit from the
BBC in 2012 cited the mostly vacant city as proof "that the great
Chinese building boom . . . is over." In his book *Ghost Cities of
China*, however, Wade Shepard argues this eulogy is premature,
pointing out that many of these cities are designed to fill up on
twenty-year timelines, and that expecting them to populate
overnight is a failure to understand China's model of urbanization—one in which the city generates population, rather than
the other way around.

Shepard recently returned to Ordos Kangbashi and found
"a substantial population there," thanks to aggressive social
engineering on the part of the Chinese authorities. In 2006,
the administrative capital of the local government was relocated there from Dongsheng, another urban area twenty miles
away. According to the *New York Times*, bus service between

the two areas was then allegedly shut down, forcing government officials to move near their offices in Kangbashi. Desirable schools were relocated to Kangbashi. Lo and behold, a city with space for 300,000 residents had become one-third full. As Shepard points out, the Chinese government has a multitude of tools that it can use to entice citizens into new cities, "shifting the population around the country as a military commander maneuvers troops on a battlefield," he writes.

One Belt One Road aims to replicate China's domestic successes in urbanization and high-speed rail in other countries around the world. But in Forest City and other offshore Chinese developments, many of the countermeasures China has used to create success at home won't be available. As we were leaving Forest City, Fancy stopped me at the door, not to deliver a final hard sell, but simply to make sure my short visit had been a pleasant one. Then she wrote her Whatsapp number on a glossy brochure and handed it to me. "Let me know when you're ready to purchase your property at Forest City," she smiled, "or at any of our other communities."

Limited Service

In 2011, Thailand was anointed an upper-middle income country, earning it a World Bank shout-out as "one of the great development success stories." Coups and floods failed to knock "Teflon Thailand" off this economic glidepath, which has been closely tethered to China's since that country opened for business in the 1970s. When Deng Xiaoping liberalized China's economy, one of Thailand's biggest private companies, Charoen Pokphand, was the first offshore enterprise to walk through the door. (Its foreign registration number on its Shenzhen SEZ investment certificate is "0001.") The countries established diplomatic ties in 1975, and bolstered these ties with mutually lucrative economic perks—like "friendship prices" for Chinese fuel sold to Thai distributors—launching an era of robust trade relations that continues to this day.

Since then, the two countries have only grown closer. In 2010, China surpassed the U.S. to become Thailand's largest

84   export market. Two years later, it replaced Japan as Thailand's biggest trading partner. A free trade agreement zeroed out tariffs on over two hundred fruits and vegetables, spiking Thai agricultural exports to jackfruit- and durian-obsessed Chinese consumers. China, in turn, has flown millions upon millions of tourists to Thai beaches and brothels, doubling country-to-country air traffic and making Bangkok the most visited city on earth.

In 2013, Chinese Premier Li Keqiang flew to Bangkok to publicly inaugurate a high-speed train exhibition with Thailand's then-Prime Minister Yingluck Shinawatra. The Chinese press covered the event as if it were a ceremonial groundbreaking, even though it was no such thing. Li called the not-yet-existent railway "a new highlight in bilateral relations."

But seven months later, Yingluck was under armed supervision at an army camp north of Bangkok, and General Prayuth Chan-ocha was sitting in the prime minister's chair.

Thailand's regime changes are a source of frustration for Beijing. Negotiations on projects must restart with each new incoming administration, and the junta put the country's major infrastructure projects on hold pending further review. Not until January 2015 did the military government breathe new life into the scheme. Prayuth announced the railway would break ground by September and that train cars would roll within two-and-a-half years. But when September arrived, talks with China had not produced terms the Thais could live with.

In December, the *Bangkok Post* reported construction would begin "as planned" in May the next year. "Bangkok Set to Be

China's Rail Hub," read the headline. (Not Thailand's rail hub— China's.) Again, the big day came and went. Over a dozen bilateral meetings have failed to resolve questions over funding, loan conditions, and divisions of labor. Ruth Banomyong, the head of the department of international business, logistics, and transport at Bangkok's Thammasat University, says the impasse comes down to a fundamental difference in governing.

"In China, it's basically a matter of, we want to do this project, so you have to do it," Banomyong says. "In Thailand, it's a little more complicated. You have to go through a number of processes: environmental, social, health impact assessments. You have to look at financial returns. This is all very foreign to the Chinese way of thinking." For instance, China operates most of its own high-speed rail lines at a loss. But Banomyong learned that when China sent the Thais the projected rate of return it had calculated for the railway, the Thai team responded that it was too low, and only a minimum of 11 or 12 percent could justify the project. Shortly thereafter, the Chinese number-crunchers came back with a new feasibility study showing a new projected rate of return: 12.1 percent. "It's a very different paradigm," says Banomyong. "A different way of working."

These differences have sometimes strained trust between the Thai and Chinese governments, which is part of why the railway project has faced multiple delays. But the bigger reason may be that Thailand simply doesn't need the railway as much as China does. Thailand is more interested in expanding passenger service, whereas China, for all its talk about a Pan-Asia bullet train, is primarily looking to move freight. And in the

86   Southeast Asia jigsaw puzzle, Thailand is the piece China simply can't afford to lose—it's an unavoidable component of any land route to Singapore.

China also wants rail access to the Gulf of Thailand's well-placed deep-sea ports, particularly in the Thai-Chinese Rayong Industrial Zone. Established in 2006, the zone is a joint venture between the Holley Group, a Chinese manufacturing conglomerate, and Amata, a Thai developer of industrial parks. It's essentially a Chinatown for heavy industry—a Forest City for factories—strewn with Chinese manufacturing plants churning out everything from solar panels to rubber products.

Rayong is one of three provinces that make up Thailand's Eastern Economic Corridor, a 5,000-square-mile "manufacturing paradise," in the words of one stakeholder. China sees the EEC as a One Belt One Road must-have. Until recently, the zone has mostly been a base for electronics, automotive, and petrochemical interests. But the Thai government wants to move the EEC further up the value chain, cultivating innovation-driven industries like robotics, aviation, medical sciences, and biofuels.

To achieve this, the government is offering huge incentives to foreign investors in the EEC, like few-strings-attached ninety-nine-year land leases and 50 percent deductions on corporate taxes. There's nothing inherently wrong with this—softening the rules for investors to spur growth in a particular region is exactly what special economic zones are designed to do. But the incentives being offered in the EEC have struck some experts as straining the limits of what's good for Thailand, or even what's considered legal under Thai law. One academic

compared the EEC to "Hong Kong in the colonial era"—a give-
away to foreign powers. Another warned that the watered-down
regulations could spark a string of foreign land grabs.

"You can do what you want here," one Chinese tourist draining
happy-hour Singhas at an outdoor bar in Bangkok told me.
"In China, there's so much pressure. You work all the time.
Everyone I know seems unhappy. Then you come to Thailand
and it's like—" he spreads his arms wide, closes his eyes, turns
his face toward the sun and smiles.

In the UN's 2017 World Happiness Report, Thailand ranked
32nd on the list, the second-happiest country in Asia after Singapore. China came in 79th, a notch above Pakistan, but an
improvement from 2012, when it ranked 112th (out of 156) and
Beijing's censors banned the report.

During this time, the number of Chinese looking for a tem-
porary escape has exploded. Virtually every one of Bangkok's
tourist attractions, malls, food stores, and duty-free shops is
awash in Chinese visitors. And Thailand has been more than
willing to welcome them, as long as they go back home after
leaving behind as much baht as possible. An easy three-hour
flight from China's southern cities, Thailand has strict laws
designed to discourage foreigners from coming in and snapping
up jobs and real estate. It's illegal for foreigners to own land in
Thailand, or to even own more than half of the units in a condo
building (since this would ostensibly make the land beneath the
building "foreign-owned.") Likewise, companies in Thailand
generally have to employ four Thais for every foreigner they hire.

In the EEC, not only are these rules being relaxed, but unprecedented incentives to lure more foreigners from China and elsewhere are being cemented into place. The government is offering foreigners the right to majority ownership of certain business sectors in the zone and relaxing the rules around long-term land leases. Many of the rule revisions were achieved through the invocation of Article 44, which gives General Prayuth absolute power to make decrees that "strengthen public unity and harmony."

In this case, Article 44 is being invoked in the name of foreign investment, a tacit acknowledgment that Thailand's economy is troubled enough to merit drastic measures. In 2013, amid political discord, growth plummeted from 6.5 percent to 2.9 percent. In 2014, it fell even further, slipping just below 1 percent. Growth has since inched up—it reached 3.2 percent in 2016—but without a solid economy, the junta knows its autocratic rule could quickly start to wear thin.

Eager to stimulate growth, bolster its standing with Beijing, and legitimize its continued place at the helm of Thailand's government, the ruling regime is creaking open the door to the railway once again. On July 11, 2017, Thailand's cabinet approved a new agreement. Using Thai construction firms and Chinese engineering, the countries agreed to build the first segment of a railway that could eventually link China to Bangkok and the EEC. Thailand is putting up over $5 billion to build phase one, money it will source both at home and overseas—including, perhaps, from the AIIB and China itself. General Prayuth again invoked Article 44 to ease restrictions on Chinese engineers who might one day work on the project.

As usual, China is framing the project as a win-win-win for all involved. The Pan-Asia Railway is really a mechanism for China to realize an array of desires in Southeast Asia. From supply chains to construction contracts, real estate ventures to coastal access, diplomatic leverage to natural resources, there's so much for China to mine from the region. Perhaps this is why it's put up with the Sisyphean setbacks for years, patiently pushing forward as its unruly neighbors to the south repeatedly capsize its carefully laid plans. If only they would stop with the protests and politics, the demands for environmental impact reports and cost-benefit projections, and simply get on board.

Epilogue

Retirement is a form of reinvention, and six months into his, Somsavat Lengsavad showed up at Wat Phon Phao on a cloudy Sunday in July. As Buddhist temples go, Wat Phon Phao is a modest one, a small peach octagon atop a scrubby, inconspicuous hill near the eastern edge of Luang Prabang. Its flaking exterior paint has been nonchalantly patched over, but its perch commanded an impressive view of the lazy Nam Khan River and the new international airport beyond.

Somsavat was there to be ordained as a monk, and from where he stood he could watch Lao Airlines turboprops alighting noisily on the tarmac below. The former statesman had stood on that tarmac three years earlier, when he presided over the airport's completion ceremony with executives from CAMC Engineering, the Chinese state-owned enterprise that built it.

His decision to return to his hometown monastery wasn't all that odd. He was seventy-one, and retired Lao politicians sometimes seek atonement at the conclusion of their careers. Somsavat's had been more consequential than most. He had set in motion a chain of events that had allowed a massive foreign entity unprecedented access to his tiny, relatively powerless nation. As he entered Wat Phon Phao at the unofficial end of his political life, hundreds of workers were pushing the first and so far only segment of the Pan-Asia Railway through Laos. For China, the segment was important, but ultimately a single part of a much larger effort. For Laos, however, it was the biggest thing to crash into the country since the Vietnam War.

"China seems to have too much investment, but it needs so much more." That's how Chinese urbanization chronicler Tom Miller put it in his book *China's Urban Billion.* To keep growing, China must keep building, if not at home then in other countries. Domestically it's struggled with a glut of development. But beyond its borders it's just getting started. Only about 35 percent of overseas lending from the country's two big policy banks is currently going to One Belt One Road investments. There's still plenty of room to grow.

The pursuit of a railway network tethering Southeast Asia to Yunnan Province offers a hint of the challenges China faces in pushing that expansion forward. China has shown it can build in Southeast Asia; its bridges, dams, and stadiums are everywhere. But Southeast Asia is a churning region, chronically awash in political upheaval, economic volatility, populist zeal, and cultural friction. The very qualities that have helped China gain entry—dysfunction, corruption, poverty—are also

92   the qualities that can turn large-scale, long-term projects into mazes with no exit. To a degree, China can turn these conditions to its advantage, but Southeast Asia is still exotic terrain for a country used to building in the hyper-controlled comfort of home. Slicing a railway through an assertive, erratic jumble of sovereign states requires recalibration, particularly when some of those states distrust your motives, fear your influence, or resent the way you do business.

China has a history defying its skeptics, however, and it's trying to learn from its mistakes. Historically, it's been a kingdom that eschewed alliances and was hesitant to embrace intimate friends. But as a rising player on the international stage, it has little choice but to engage, and building infrastructural and commercial links is the tactic it's chosen for reaching out to the world. This has resulted in spectacular Chinese-led development projects abroad, and years from now, a rail network running the length of the Malay Peninsula may be included on that roster of achievements. "Development," as President Xi Jinping unabashedly said in his opening remarks at the Belt and Road Forum in 2017, "holds the master key to solving all problems."

There's a gulf between China's reality and how it depicts itself to the world. When its economic data is insufficiently impressive, the government simply modifies the numbers. It hides its slums behind false facades during international events, and varnishes up the most innocuous bit of news that doesn't reflect an ideal PRC. So it's no surprise Beijing has put the best possible face on its Pan-Asia Railway, with press

releases, promotional videos, and ceremonial groundbreakings
celebrating its dawn.

The outcome China craves isn't a one-seat ride from Kunming to Singapore. It's a region infused with Chinese influence, connections, and control. Along with the highways, pipelines, and economic zones China is establishing across Southeast Asia, a Pan-Asia Railway would draw a coveted part of the world further into the Sinosphere. But China's long, awkward journey to this point highlights the daunting task that is ahead.

Acknowledgments

I've wanted to write this story for quite some time, and I'm grateful to Jimmy So, Nick Lemann, Camille McDuffie, and the rest of the team at Columbia Global Reports for allowing me to do so. Jimmy, in particular, was an ever-present source of brilliant ideas and insightful critiques, delivered and debated over cups of coffee, bowls of pho, and rounds of ping-pong.

In Laos, I worked with several locals who were generous with their time and trust, most of whom cannot be named here due to that country's laws against legitimate journalism. One who did give me permission to thank him is Sengphouxay "Seng" Inthavikham, who guided me through the remote Lao-China border region and helped me earn the trust of the people I met there. Callan Cheng, the young man from Kunming working in Boten, was one of those people, and I appreciate his willingness to let a perfect stranger intrude on his daily life.

In Singapore, I owe debts of gratitude to Ed Baker and Dan Gerrella at Broadway Malyan, Jordan Schwartz at the World Bank, and author Parag Khanna. The research staff at ISEAS patiently walked me through the eccentricities of Singaporean urban planning. Lucas Yong was a delightful accomplice as my fellow "condo buyer" in Malaysia.

In Yangon and Chiang Mai, the reporters and editors at *Democratic Voice of Burma* were kind enough to let me wander the newsroom and interrupt them with questions as they worked to meet their deadlines. In Bangkok, Sipat Vongsakul was an invaluable translator, fixer, and friend, and contributed more cumulative hours to this project than perhaps anyone other than me and my editor.

Agatha Kratz, who has studied virtually every aspect of the Pan-Asia Railway, read drafts of this book in its entirety; her feedback, corrections, and encouragement transformed the final product. Many other readers reviewed sections of early drafts as well, which led to substantive improvements to both individual chapters and the overall premise. Those people are David Roberts, Brian Eyler, Frank Albert, Vicky Bowman, Termsak Chalermpalanupap, Cassey Lee, Simon Creak, and Mary Kay Magistad.

Finally, thank you to my parents and family for always being supportive, particularly Tom Mulkern, Sr., who started encouraging me to become a journalist from the time I was a child. And most of all, to my loving partner and effective teammate Ben Donner, for his limitless enthusiasm for projects like these.

FURTHER READING

Sebastian Strangio, *Hun Sen's Cambodia* (Yale University Press, 2014). Sebastian Strangio's immersive biography of a career dictator and his crackpot Chinese client state is a case study in gonzo Southeast Asian politics. It's also a cautionary tale for Laos, which, like Cambodia, risks becoming consumed by Chinese debt. More than a biography, it's an exhaustive indictment of the cynical profiteering that defines so much development in this region of the world.

Evan Osnos, *Age of Ambition: Chasing Fortune, Truth, and Faith in the New China* (Farrar, Straus and Giroux, 2014). Evan Osnos hardly needs a recommendation from me. He's one of the most read—and most readable—voices writing about China today. *Age of Ambition*, which draws on some of his past reporting for *The New Yorker,* teases out the exuberance and anxiety of a country that seems just as caught off guard by its sudden ascent as the rest of the world.

Leslie T. Chang, *Factory Girls: From Village to City in a Changing China* (Spiegel & Grau, 2008). China's rising power has been cultivated through the sweat of a massive migrant labor force. Leslie T. Chang provides an often harrowing account of the lives of a few of the young women who serve in this army of itinerant workers. Their stories reveal the range of sacrifices individuals must make in order to achieve not only their own ambitions, but those of their society.

Orville Schell and John Delury, *Wealth and Power: China's Long March to the Twenty-first Century* (Random House, 2013). Why did China rise to become a world superpower? To the extent this question can be answered, John Delury and Orville Schell chronicle China's centuries-long pursuit of *fuqiang*: wealth and power. By reaching deep into the past, a wide-angle view of China's trajectory emerges, making its current surge in power seem practically predestined.

Paul Theroux, *The Great Railway Bazaar: By Train Through Asia*   99
(Houghton Mifflin, 1975). Four decades ago the world's crankiest traveler
took a series of trains through Asia, and today, most of those rail systems
are just as decrepit, or worse. But what's most striking about Theroux's
account is how little some parts of the Southeast Asian countryside
outside of its booming major cities have developed since then, which
China's presence may change in the coming years.

Sinica and *Ear to Asia* podcasts. Produced by SupChina and the University
of Melbourne's Asia Institute, respectively, *Sinica* and *Ear to Asia* provide
smart, digestible insights in podcast form. *Sinica* is the more irreverent
of the two—it's co-hosted by a self-described member of China's first
heavy metal band.

Yu Hua, *China in Ten Words* (Anchor Books, 2012). Banned in China,
Yu Hua's account of his upbringing during the Cultural Revolution is
mesmerizing. Viewed through the eyes of a child who has known nothing
else, Mao Zedong's maniacal reign seems almost normal.

Mike Davis, *City of Quartz: Excavating the Future in Los Angeles* (Verso,
1990). This deep dive into the slums, mini-malls, and gated communities
of 1980s Los Angeles is awash with the presence of Japan, a country most
people (the author included) assumed would own much of California by
now. China is barely mentioned in its pages, which is why I include it on
this list—as an artifact of a moment when the world was looking in one
direction while the future crept in from another.

NOTES

INTRODUCTION

12 when Shanghai decided to build a subway, the World Bank scolded it: "Staff Appraisal Report: Shanghai Metropolitan Transport Project," The World Bank. http://documents.worldbank.org/curated/en/613241468241456536/text/multiopage.txt

12 its Tunnel Engineering Bureau dug a prototype 2,100-foot tunnel and metro station: "The Shanghai No. 1 Subway Line," *Japan Railway & Transport Review*, January 1997.

13 "Shanghai, it seems, is eager to play catch-up with the rest of the world": Seth Faison, "Shanghai Journal; Free Now to Build, China's Biggest City Binges," *New York Times*, April 12, 1995.

14 a fifty-seven-story skyscraper in nineteen days: Finn Aberdein, "Chairman Zhang's Flatpack Skyscrapers," BBC, June 11, 2015.

17 a massive network of tracks Paul Theroux dubbed the Iron Rooster: Paul Theroux, *Riding the Iron Rooster: By Train Through China*, G.P. Putnam's Sons, 1988.

18 the annual $1.7 trillion in infrastructure developing Asia needs: "Meeting Asia's Infrastructure Needs," Asian Development Bank. https://www.adb.org/sites/default/files/publication/227496/special-report-infrastructure-highlights.pdf

20 Boten was essentially a Chinese city: Sebastian Strangio, "The Rise, Fall and Possible Renewal of a Town in Laos on China's Border," *New York Times*, July 6, 2016.

21 the U.S. State Department suspected this company might be "a front organization": "China's Golden City in Northern Laos," Wikileaks, March 20, 2007. https://wikileaks.org/plusd/cables/07VIENTIANE228_a.html

22 Overwhelmed Lao immigration officials: ibid.

23 The Asian Development Bank managed the project: "New Overland Route Links Singapore to Beijing," Asian Development Bank. https://www.adb.org/news/new-overland-route-links-singapore-beijing

23 the headline failing to even mention little Laos: "China to Build Highway to Link China and Thailand," *People's Daily*, February 8, 2002.

23 "Half the people were throwing up": Thomas Fuller, "In Isolated Hills of Asia, New Roads to Speed Trade," *New York Times*, March 31, 2008.

24 it had exploded to $154 billion: Francois Bafoil, *Emerging Capitalism in Central Europe and Southeast Asia*, Palgrave MacMillan, 2014.

25 the twenty-fifth annual Southeast Asian Games: Simon

102   Creak, "Sport as Politics and History," *Anthropology Today*, February 2011. http://www.newmandala.org/wp-content/uploads/2012/04/Creak-2011-SEA-Games.pdf

26   **build the $100 million facility on one condition:** Martin Stuart-Fox, "Laos: The Chinese Connection," *Southeast Asian Affairs*, 2009.

26   **At a press conference in February 2008:** "China Land Deal Rankles Laos Capital," by Reuters Staff, Reuters, April 6, 2008. https://www.reuters.com/article/idUSBKK243478

27   **The That Luang complex was downsized in 2010:** "Vientiane Authorities Say That Luang Area Belongs to Investors," by RFA's Lao Service, Radio Free Asia, August 1, 2013. https://www.rfa.org/english/news/laos/concessions-080120 13161959.html

29   **a communist insurgency known as the Pathet Lao:** Grant Evans, *A Short History of Laos*, Allen & Unwin, 2002.

30   **Laos's goal was to get its hydropower generation:** "Powering Up the Battery of Southeast Asia," GE Reports, October 5, 2016. https://www.ge.com/reports/powering-up-the-battery-of-southeast-asia/

31   **Laos was an insular kingdom:** ibid.

32   **"Frankly speaking, the ministerial reshuffle has slowed down the project":** Peter Janssen, "Laos High-Speed Rail Plan Delayed," *Bangkok Post*, May 4, 2011.

34   **unable to pay its civil servants on time:** Ounkeo Souksavanh, "Salary Delays Slow Government Work in Laos," Radio Free Asia, January 6, 2017. https://www.rfa.org/english/news/laos/delays-01062017142322.html

35   **over nine million acres of Laotian land:** "Laos Corruption Report," GAN Business Anti-Corruption Portal. https://www.business-anti-corruption.com/country-profiles/laos

36   **corruption had cost Laos $120 million:** "Former Lao Finance Minister Named in Corruption Probe," RFA's Lao Service, Radio Free Asia, January 8, 2016. https://www.rfa.org/english/news/laos/corruption-01082016142933.html

36   **ranking Laos the world's fifty-first most corrupt state:** "Corruption Perceptions Index 2016," Transparency International. https://www.transparency.org/news/feature/corruption_perceptions_index_2016

39   **Chinese Foreign Minister Wang Yi arrived in Laos:** Press Release, Ministry of Foreign Affairs of the People's Republic of China, April 24, 2016. http://www.fmprc.gov.cn/mfa_eng/zxxx_662805/t1358480.shtml

CHAPTER TWO

43   **The route will require:** "Fears for Little Laos under China's Kunming-to-Singapore Rail Vision," *Global Construction Review*, January 22, 2014. http://www.global

constructionreview.com/sectors/
fears-little-laos-under-chinas-
kunming-singapore-r/

**44 a 2012 memo put out by the
Chinese embassy in Nairobi:**
He Wenping, "China-Africa
Economic Relations: Current
Situation and Future Challenges,
Infrastructure as an Example,"
China-Africa Partnership. https://
issuu.com/irenkenya/docs/
china-africa_partnership_pdf

**47 "remarkably quiet border
crossing":** "Yunnan's Border
Trade," Wikileaks, February 26,
2010. https://wikileaks.org/
plusd/cables/10CHENGDU46_
a.html

**47 approaching half a trillion
dollars per year:** "Towards a Closer
ASEAN-China Community of
Shared Future," Ministry of Foreign
Affairs of the People's Republic of
China, July 14, 2017. http://www.
fmprc.gov.cn/mfa_eng/wjb_663304/
zwjg_665342/zwbd_665378/
t1477905.shtml

CHAPTER THREE

**52 $10 billion per year on its soft
power programs:** David Shambaugh,
"China's Soft-Power Push," *Foreign
Affairs*, July/August 2015.

**53 an annual average of 11
percent:** David Dollar, "China's
Rise as a Regional and Global
Power," Brookings Institute. https://
www.brookings.edu/research/
chinas-rise-as-a-regional-and-
global-power-the-aiib-and-the-
one-belt-one-road/

**54 roughly half of its GDP on
these types of investments:** Kelsey
Wilkins and Andrew Zurawski,
"Infrastructure Investment in
China," *Bulletin*, June 2014. https://
www.rba.gov.au/publications/
bulletin/2014/jun/pdf/bu-0614-
4.pdf

**55 41 percent of global rail
revenues:** "China's High-Speed Rail
Diplomacy," U.S.-China Economic
and Security Review Commission.
https://www.uscc.gov/sites/default/
files/Research/China%27s%20
High%20Speed%20Rail%20
Diplomacy.pdf

**55 over $100 million lower than
the closest competitor's:** Nicole
Dungca, "Losing Bidder Wants
Chinese Train Builder Disqualified,"
Boston Globe, November 8, 2014.

**55 CRRC representative An
Zhongyi thanked the crowd:**
Spencer Buell, "The MBTA's Orange
Line Mockup Is at City Hall," *Boston
Magazine*, September 3, 2017.
http://www.bostonmagazine.com/
news/2017/04/03/mbta-orange-line-
mockup-city-hall/

**56 magnanimously put it in a
2017 interview:** Kevin P. Gallagher,
"China's influence on global finance
grows as US scales back input,"
Financial Times, March 27, 2017.

**56 China's outbound investment
flows:** "China Outbound Investment
Surges Past $100 Billion," AFP,
January 16, 2015. http://gulfnews.
com/business/economy/china-
outbound-investment-surges-past-
100-billion-1.1442400

104   **57   156 countries and regions:**
"China Now a Net Capital Exporter,"
Xinhua, January 21, 2015. http://
www.chinadaily.com.cn/business/
chinadata/2015-01/21/content_1936
7818.htm

**57   Mao told the leaders of both
countries:** David Abdulai, *Chinese
Investment in Africa*, Routledge, 2017.

58   Kenyatta said proudly: "Kenya
Opens Nairobi-Mombasa Madaraka
Express Railway," BBC, May 31,
2017. http://www.bbc.com/news/
world-africa-40092600

**58   the World Bank declined to
finance the project in 2013:** "The
Economics of Rail Gauge in the East
Africa Community," The World Bank.
https://www.theelephant.info/
documents/world-bank-report-the-
economics-of-rail-gauge-in-the-
east-african-community/

59   Fitch Ratings released a report:
"Fitch: China's One Belt, One Road
Initiative Brings Risks," Reuters
Staff, Reuters, January 25, 2017.
https://www.reuters.com/article/
idUSFit987609

**59   A press release from the
State Council of China:** "Top
Spokesman Premiere Li Promotes
China's High-Speed Rail," The
State Council, The People's
Republic of China. http://english.
gov.cn/premier/news/2015/12/29/
content_281475262862422.htm

60   a sharkbite 6.3 percent: "China
-Sri Lanka Strategic Hambantota
Port Deal," National Maritime
Foundation, April 13, 2017. http://
www.maritimeindia.org/View%20
Profile/636276610966827339.pdf

**60   reportedly hired to prevent
local wildlife:** Brook Larmer, "What
the World's Emptiest International
Airport Says about Chinese
Influence," *New York Times Magazine*,
September 13, 2017.

**60   Sri Lanka agreed to give
Beijing:** Ranga Sirilal, "Sri Lanka to
Hand Port to Chinese Firm, Receive
$300 Million," Reuters, December
5, 2017. https://in.reuters.com/
article/sri-lanka-china-ports/
sri-lanka-to-hand-port-to-
chinese-firm-receive-300-million-
idINKBN1E003K

61   with one scholar: Brahma
Chellaney, "China's Debt-Trap
Diplomacy," LiveMint, January 27,
2017. http://www.livemint.com/
Opinion/21P46wlPXj00K8VUKMu90
N/Chinas-debttrap-diplomacy.html

62   A BMI Research report: Kamran
Haider and Chris Kay, "Pakistan
Dismissed Chinese Debt-Trap
Concerns," Bloomberg, January 29,
2017. https://www.bloomberg.com/
news/articles/2017-01-29/chinese-
debt-trap-concern-dismissed-by-
pakistan-as-gdp-quickens

63   "It's back to the future": Jim
Kinney, "Rail Car Maker CRRC
MA Sends Workers to China
for Training," MassLive, April 7,
2017. http://www.masslive.com/
business-news/index.ssf/2017/04/
rail_car_maker_crrc_ma_sends_
workers_to.html

**63   a relatively large, healthy,
literate workforce:** David Leonhardt,
"In China, Cultivating the Urge to
Splurge," *New York Times Magazine*,
November 24, 2010.

65   **topping $50 billion in 2016:** "China Remains as Malaysia's Largest Trading Partner in 2015," Xinhua, February 6, 2016. http://www.chinadaily. com.cn/business/2016-02/06/ content_23415083.htm

CHAPTER FOUR

66   **a vast expansion of the capital:** Bandar Malaysia brochure. http://www.bandarmalaysia.my/ wp-content/uploads/2015/09/ BM_TeaserBrochure.pdf

66   **which began taking shape in 2011:** "Six Vying to be Bandar Malaysia Designer Instead of Five," TheEdge, May 17, 2012. http:// www.theedgemarkets.com/article/ six-vying-be-bandar-malaysia- designer-instead-five

67   **At a signing ceremony on December 13, 2016:** Royston Sim, "Historic Agreement for Singapore- Kuala Lumpur High-Speed Rail Signed," *Straits Times*, December 14, 2016.

67   **already secured the contract for another Malaysian rail link:** Eva Grey, "China Turns Malaysia's East Coast Rail Link into Reality," *Railway Technology*, October 1, 2017. https://www.railway-technology. com/features/featurechina-turns- malaysias-east-coast-rail-link- into-reality-5938409/

68   **a Chinese envoy embraced his country's usual sales pitch:** "China Railway Showcases High-Speed Rail Mock-Up in Kuala Lumpur," *Straits Times*, January 17, 2017.

68   **first overseas railcar factory in Malaysia's Perak State:** Keith Barrow, "CRRC Opens Malaysian Rolling Stock Plant," *International Railway Journal*, July 13, 2015. http:// www.railjournal.com/index.php/ asia/crrc-opens-malaysian-rolling- stock-plant.html

68   **"best ever":** Keith Zhai and Pooi Koon Chong, "China Wants This Port to Rival Singapore (and That's Not All)," Bloomberg, July 31, 2017. https://www.bloomberg.com/ news/articles/2017-07-31/chinese- money-pouring-into-malaysia- could-help-najib-razak-with -votes

69   **pour another $2 billion into the property:** "China's CREC to Set Up US$2B Regional Centre in Bandar Malaysia," CRECM Press Release. https://crec.com.my/chinas-crec- set-us2b-regional-centre-bandar- malaysia/

69   **"Bandar Malaysia Has Become Bandar China":** FinanceTwitter, October 27, 2016. http://www. financetwitter.com/2016/10/ bandar-malaysia-has-become- bandar-china-the-united-states- malays-conned-by-najib.html

69   **top of its foreign investor list:** Amy Chew, "China Becomes Malaysia's Biggest Foreign Investor, Thanks to 1MDB Purchases," *South China Morning Post*, January 12, 2016.

70   **a ponzi scheme:** "Swiss Request Further Assistance from Malaysia in 1MDB Case," AFP, October 5, 2016. http://www. straitstimes.com/asia/se-asia/

106   swiss-request-further-assistance-
       from-malaysia-in-1mdb-case

70   **"largest kleptocracy case":**
"U.S. Seeks to Recover $1 Billion in
Largest Kleptocracy Case to Date,"
FBI, July 20, 2016. https://www.
fbi.gov/news/stories/us-seeks-
to-recover-1-billion-in-largest-
kleptocracy-case-to-date

70   **Najib himself was accused:**
Tom Wright and Simon Clark,
"Investigators Believe Money
Flowed to Malaysian Leader Najib's
Accounts Amid 1MDB Probe," *Wall
Street Journal*, July 2, 2015.

70   **a Chinese "bailout":** "China to
Help 1MDB Settle Multi-Billion-
Dollar Legal Dispute with Abu Dhabi:
Financial Times," *Straits Times*,
December 7, 2016.

70   **despaired a Japanese executive:**
Leslie Lopez, "China, Japan Jostle
for Lead Role in Singapore-KL Rail
Project," *Straits Times*, April 12, 2016.

70   **claiming the contract was
canceled:** "Malaysia's $1.7 Billion
Property Deal to Cut 1MDB Debt
Falls Through," Reuters, May 3, 2017.

70   **The consortium disputed this:**
ibid.

71   **dipped below $3 trillion:**
Lingling Wei, "China's Foreign
Exchange Reserves Drop Below $3
Trillion, Near Six-Year Low," *Wall
Street Journal*, February 7, 2017.

71   **pen a defensive op-ed:** Najib
Razak, "Why Malaysia Supports
China's Belt and Road," *South China
Morning Post*, May 12, 2017.

71   **announcing a fresh push:** Tho
Xin Yi, "Japan Raises Efforts to Win
High Speed Rail Project," *The Star*,
May 5, 2017.

CHAPTER FIVE

75   **"like a Chinatown":** Johan
Nylander, "Troubles in Malaysia's
Forest City Paradise," *Asia Times*,
May 6, 2017.

76   **44 percent of the visa's
successful applicants:** Tashny
Sukumaran and Coco Liu, "Why Are
Chinese Moving to Malaysia by the
Thousands?" *South China Morning
Post*, March 25, 2017.

76   **"a strong and sustainable
metropolis":** Iskandar Regional
Development Authority. http://
www.irda.com.my/about-us/

79   **outspoken in his alarm:**
"FDI," Tun Dr Mahathir Mohamad,
January 9, 2017. http://mahathir-
mohamad.blogspot.com/2017/01/
fdi.html

79   **as the anthropologist Chris
Lyttleton calls them:** Chris
Lyttleton and Pal Nyiri, "Dams,
Casinos and Concessions: Chinese
Megaprojects in Laos and Cambodia,"
Engineering Earth, eds. Stanley D.
Brunn, Springer: Dordrecht, 2011.

80   **$33 billion in offshore real
estate:** Ellen Sheng, "Chinese
Investment in Overseas Real Estate
Hit Record High in 2016," *Forbes*,
January 31, 2017.

80   **closed "for renovations":**
"China Capital Curbs Force $100

Billion Forest City to Seek Buyers Elsewhere," Reuters, March 31, 2017.

81   **the BBC in 2012:** Peter Day, "Ordos: The Biggest Ghost Town in China," *BBC Magazine*, March 17, 2012.

81   **Shepard recently returned to Ordos Kangbashi:** Wade Shepard, "How Universities Are Used to Stimulate Growth in China's Ghost Cities," Vagabond Journey, January 25, 2016. https://www.vagabondjourney.com/how-universities-are-used-to-stimulate-growth-in-chinas-ghost-cities/

81   **bus service between the two areas:** Jody Rosen, "The Colossal Strangeness of China's Most Excellent Tourist City," *New York Times Style Magazine*, March 6, 2015.

CHAPTER SIX

84   **Bangkok the most visited city on earth:** Global Destination Cities Index. https://newsroom.mastercard.com/wp-content/uploads/2016/09/Global-Destination-Cities-Index-Report.pdf

87   **"Hong Kong in the colonial era":** Oliver Ward, "Thailand's Eastern Economic Corridor - Will This Be Another Failed Project in ASEAN?" ASEAN Today, May 27, 2017. https://www.aseantoday.com/2017/05/thailands-eastern-economic-corridor-will-this-be-another-failed-project-in-asean%EF%BC%9F/

87   **UN's 2017 World Happiness Report:** World Happiness Report 2017. http://worldhappiness.report/wp-content/uploads/sites/2/2017/03/HR17.pdf

88   **Thailand's cabinet approved a new agreement:** "Thailand Greenlights First Phase of $5.5 Billion Railway Project With China," Reuters, July 11, 2017.

EPILOGUE

90   **he presided over the airport's completion ceremony:** "CAMC Engineering Laos Luang Prabang International Airport Reconstruction Project Completed," Press Release, Sinomach, September 25, 2013. http://www.sinomach.com.cn/en/MediaCenter/News/201412/t20141209_22068.html

91   **Only about 35 percent:** David Dollar, "Yes, China Is Investing Globally—But Not So Much In Its Belt and Road Initiative," Brookings Institute, May 8, 2017. https://www.brookings.edu/blog/order-from-chaos/2017/05/08/yes-china-is-investing-globally-but-not-so-much-in-its-belt-and-road-initiative/

Columbia Global Reports is a publishing imprint from Columbia University that commissions authors to do original on-site reporting around the globe on a wide range of issues. The resulting novella-length books offer new ways to look at and understand the world that can be read in a few hours. Most readers are curious and busy. Our books are for them.

Subscribe to Columbia Global Reports and get six books a year in the mail in advance of publication. globalreports.columbia.edu/subscribe

2018

Pipe Dreams:
The Plundering of
Iraq's Oil Wealth
Erin Banco

Never Remember:
Searching for Stalin's
Gulags in Putin's Russia
Masha Gessen
and Misha Friedman

Saudi America:
Fracking and the New Age
of Oil, Money and Power
Bethany McLean

The Nationalist Revival:
Trade, Immigration, and the
Revolt Against Globalization
John B. Judis

The Curse of Bigness:
Antitrust in the New Gilded Age
Tim Wu

We Want to Negotiate:
The Secret World of
Kidnapping, Hostages,
and Ransom
Joel Simon